I0773919

Secrets & Shortcuts

A Rogue's Handbook of Unethical Life Hacks

WRITTEN BY: Darius Xavier

PUBLISHED BY: Black Grimoire Press

Table of Contents

Introduction

Welcome to Secrets & Shortcuts: A Rogue's Handbook of Unethical Life Hacks. If you're holding this book, chances are you've sensed that the world doesn't play entirely fair. The everyday landscape, your job, your bills, the red tape, the endless promotions that never quite deliver, can feel rigged. It's not that you're failing; it's that the game is rigged against the honest and the well-intentioned. Truthfully, plenty of people are working an angle, cutting a corner, or quietly bending the rules. They're the ones who always seem to land the upgrade, snag the last freebie, or slip out of trouble at the last second.

This is a guidebook to their world. It's a toolkit for those who've glimpsed the back door to the system and want a closer look. We'll be pulling back the curtain on tactics that range from morally gray to outright unscrupulous, but all designed to give you the upper hand in everyday situations. From saving money in sneaky ways to gently pressuring institutions for a better deal, these chapters aim to sharpen your instincts, hone your opportunism, and embolden your approach.

But let's state the obvious: this isn't a polite, "feel-good" self-improvement manifesto. You won't find life-affirming mottos here, nor sunny affirmations about following your dreams. Instead, you'll discover how to identify the weaknesses and blind spots in systems and people, and how to exploit them for your gain. This is the murky territory where ethics and profit collide, where you'll ask yourself uncomfortable questions: Is this too far? What if I get caught? Is the payoff worth the pang of guilt?

We're not here to moralize. In fact, this book assumes you're already questioning the rules of a world that's built to benefit the insiders. Maybe you're tired of playing nice. Maybe you're curious how others get ahead when you seem to stall. Or maybe you just want to peek behind the scenes before deciding what kind of person you truly want to be.

Consider this your unauthorized guide to loopholes and grey zones, an arsenal of subtle tricks and strategic gambles. As you move through these pages, remember two things: First, knowledge is power, you can always choose to use these tactics sparingly, responsibly, or not at all. And second, we're all rogues to someone. In a world of quiet cheats and institutional slight-of-hand, maybe a little cunning is exactly what you need to even the odds.

Once you learn and understand these secrets and tactics; you'll never see the world the same again. **This is your last chance to turn back**.

If you're ready to change your life forever, let's get started.

Chapter 1:
Opening the Door to
Unethical Thinking

If you've picked up this book, you're likely tired of the status quo, tired of playing by rigid rules that never seem to favor you, of paying your dues and waiting your turn while others sail past you with a wink and a grin. You've probably felt the sting of playing by the book, only to watch as someone else, often less deserving, nabs the promotion, secures the upgrade, or glides through life's checkpoints with suspicious ease. It's not that you lack intelligence or capability. More likely, you lack the willingness to question the system and the nerve to seize the subtle opportunities lurking beneath everyday transactions, interactions, and agreements.

This first chapter is about pulling back the curtain on the very mindset that allows some people to consistently get ahead without putting in proportionate effort. We'll shine a light on the idea that rules, codes of conduct, and social norms, while beneficial in theory, are often full of exploitable gaps. By the time you turn the page to the next chapter, you should feel your moral compass wobble slightly as you begin to understand that the distinction between following the rules and cleverly sidestepping them is more fluid, more negotiable, than you once believed.

Acknowledging the Unspoken Rules

The Hidden Norms and Unwritten Codes:

From a young age, most of us are trained to be "good." We're taught to wait in line, take our fair share, follow directions, and apologize when we err. These lessons form the invisible skeleton of civilization. They keep things orderly and predictable, most of the time. Yet, as you grow older, you realize that many of these expectations are not rigid laws, but social conveniences. They're guidelines that help grease the wheels of society, but they aren't always enforced and often rely on voluntary compliance.

Consider, for example, how we behave in a supermarket. There's no official rule stating you must line up behind the person who arrived before you, only a custom. If you cut the line, you face disapproving glares and perhaps a confrontation, but it's not illegal. The system relies on everyone choosing to obey that norm. Now, scale that idea up: beyond the supermarket line, there are all sorts of "shoulds" that people follow without question. You "should" accept the posted price as final, you "should" take no more than one sample, you "should" follow the instructions to the letter. Most people do, and that's what makes the system stable for everyone else.

How Some People Get Ahead by Bending the Rules:

But stability can also mean stagnation, and for those with opportunistic eyes, these unwritten norms are more like helpful suggestions than binding commands. Imagine the frequent flier who strides confidently to a slightly better seat after boarding, occupying it as if it's theirs all along. Or the conference attendee who quickly pockets extra name badges to access various invite-only sessions. These people leverage the fact that most officials, clerks, and gatekeepers will not call you out if you act as though you belong. They leverage the assumed goodwill and compliance of others, using it as a springboard for personal gain.

This doesn't mean the world is full of mustache-twirling villains. Often, these opportunists justify their actions with private logic: "This airline constantly cancels flights, why not snag a better seat if I can?" or "These hotel upgrades cost the chain pennies, and I've been a loyal guest." They rationalize bending the rules as a minor corrective measure against an inherently unfair or bloated system. Understanding this mindset, that the rules are flexible when you approach them with confidence, is the first step in freeing yourself from blind compliance.

Understanding the Appeal of Shortcuts

The Psychology of Wanting Something for Nothing:

Humans are natural shortcut-takers. Evolutionarily speaking, conserving energy and securing resources efficiently was a survival advantage. Today, that instinct manifests in subtler ways. We relish a good sale, cherish buy-one-get-one deals, and gloat about snagging a discount code online. The satisfaction is not just about saving money; it's about beating the system, feeling clever, and emerging victorious in a small, everyday contest.

When these shortcuts venture into morally gray territory, like using fake names to redeem multiple free trials, our brains may still revel in the win. After all, what's the difference between that and extreme couponing? Both exploit systems designed to encourage certain behaviors. The line between clever consumer and cunning rogue can be surprisingly thin.

Minor Dishonesties That Go Unnoticed:

On a micro-scale, everyday life is rife with overlooked acts of dishonesty. Returning a worn item as if brand new, quietly pocketing an extra promotional keychain that was "one per customer," or feigning forgetfulness when asked to pay a small fee, these small transgressions often go unpunished. Why? Because nobody wants the hassle of a confrontation over trivial matters. Corporate return desks rarely challenge customers vigorously, hotels often waive minor charges to keep guests happy, and restaurants may comp a dish if you complain politely. The systems in place rely on an honor code that many take for granted. By politely violating that code, the cunning individual gains incremental advantages without drawing heat.

Consider the digital realm: signing up repeatedly for free trials with burner email accounts is a near-ubiquitous hack. Streaming platforms, online services, and software trials can be milked indefinitely if you're clever enough. It's not that the companies don't know this happens, they do. But investing resources to police each petty violator often costs more than the loss incurred. Thus, a silent détente forms: they turn a semi-blind eye, and you, the opportunist, get your goodies without fuss.

Defining "Unethical Life Hacks" in Context

Distinguishing Between Illegality and Moral Flexibility:

It's crucial to define our territory. "Unethical" does not always mean illegal. There's a wide gradient between downright criminal acts and harmless white lies. Imagine a scale: on one end is outright theft, shoplifting, embezzlement, fraud. On the other end is the squeaky-clean consumer who pays every fee, reads every contract line by line, and never deviates from stated policies. In between lies a broad expanse of questionable behavior: using ambiguous return policies to get free rentals, leveraging a friend's discount code under a different name, or slipping into a "members only" lounge without explicit permission.

The tactics we'll explore often land in this gray middle zone. They're not always clearly against the law, and even when they nudge the boundaries of legality, the risk of enforcement or penalty is low. Consider something as mundane as returning an item you purchased online by claiming a minor defect that doesn't actually bother you. You're not defrauding them in the grand sense, most companies build the cost of returns into their models, but you are manipulating the system's generosity. This isn't a legal battleground; it's an ethical quagmire, and you decide how far in you're willing to wade.

Clarifying the Goals: Getting Ahead Versus Outright Harm:

At this point, you might ask, "What's the harm?" The answer depends on your values and perspective. On one hand, most of these small hacks harm no one significantly. The company takes a negligible financial hit, a faceless institution absorbs a minor inconvenience, or an event host loses an extra canapé. On the other hand, a world where everyone bends the rules can quickly descend into chaos, forcing businesses to tighten policies, raise prices, or become more adversarial to honest customers.

While some readers might feel comfortable with small deceptions, justifying them as the cost of doing business, others will balk at even mild dishonesty. The purpose of this book isn't to coax you into committing grand acts of villainy. Instead, it aims to highlight that the world is not evenly balanced. Those who abide strictly by the letter of the law often find themselves at a disadvantage compared to those who read between the lines. Recognizing this fact doesn't mean you must exploit it, but it helps to understand the lay of the land.

Seeing the System Through New Eyes

Examining Everyday Interactions:

One of the first practical steps in adopting this new perspective is to reexamine ordinary transactions and interactions. When you order a coffee, consider how the barista's compliance, the menu's pricing structure, and the shop's promotional policies might be nudged. Could you claim a birthday reward one day early? What if you politely but firmly mention a slight bitterness in your brew, might they offer a refund or free replacement? This isn't to say you should hound small businesses for every dime, but it serves as an exercise: start noticing where the boundaries lie and who's enforcing them. By becoming aware of these implicit understandings, you train yourself to see possibilities.

Questioning Why Things Are the Way They Are:

Society presents many things as immutable facts, but in truth, they're often arbitrary guidelines. Why must you pay a $20 fee if you change your reservation date by a single day? Because someone decided that was the policy. But is that policy universally enforced, or could a well-placed appeal to a sympathetic customer service rep waive it? Many corporate rules exist more as deterrents than as absolute dogmas. If you challenge them, politely and confidently, you'll often find them malleable. The first step is learning to question the validity and applicability of these so-called "facts."

Redefining Morality in Practical Terms

From Absolutes to Gradients:

Most people are taught morality in black and white terms. It's "wrong" to lie, "wrong" to steal, and "wrong" to cheat. But life rarely fits neatly into those categories. Consider that entire industries revolve around subtle manipulation: marketing, politics, entertainment. Advertisers don't outright lie, but they certainly stretch truths and evoke emotions to influence your spending. Is that ethical? It's accepted practice, so we swallow it without much protest. Meanwhile, when an individual consumer flips the script, exploiting a loophole to gain personal advantage, society might wag a moralizing finger. This double standard should give you pause.

It's entirely possible that by exploring these tactics, you're simply leveling the playing field. After all, corporations and institutions design systems that benefit themselves. Why not tweak those systems ever so slightly to your favor? We're not encouraging you to abandon all sense of right and wrong. Instead, think of ethics as fluid guidelines that shift depending on context, scale, and consequence. If you find certain methods too distasteful, you can skip them. But having the knowledge doesn't harm you; it only expands your range of options.

Rationalizing Personal Gain:

The discomfort you might feel reading this chapter is natural. Society trains us to be good players on a team: we do our part, trust others to do theirs, and collectively benefit. When you start to embrace unethical life hacks, you risk feeling guilty, deceitful, or even predatory. Yet, remember that others have no qualms about using similar strategies. Big corporations exploit tax loopholes. Influencers fabricate glowing testimonials. Political operatives spin narratives to shape public opinion. The world is already a tapestry of half-truths and manipulations. In that sense, your mild acts of rule-bending are merely part of the broader game.

Preparing for What Lies Ahead

Building a Mindset of Strategic Opportunism:

The chapters that follow will guide you deeper into the art and science of subtle cheating. Before you delve in, internalize this key shift: you are training yourself to think differently. No longer will you accept "no" at face value. Instead, you'll ask, "What if I push a little? What if I pretend not to know the rule? What if I suggest the rule is unfair or unenforceable?" You'll learn to keep a straight face while making bold requests and to camouflage your intentions behind politeness, confusion, or manufactured urgency.

Think of yourself as an explorer charting unknown territory. The map you were given at birth showed only the main roads and lawful routes. We're about to venture onto hidden footpaths, back alleys, and secret shortcuts. These may not always be safe or pretty, but they'll open your eyes to a more flexible reality.

Setting Boundaries and Exit Strategies:

Even as you step into this world, it's prudent to set personal boundaries. Determine what lines you won't cross. Understand what consequences you're willing to risk. There's a difference between bending a return policy to get a free replacement and forging documents to secure a loan, one might feel like a harmless hack, the other a step too far. Keep your moral compass handy, even if its needle is spinning a bit. And remember that you can always step back into the light after dabbling in the shadows. Knowledge is not a contract, it's a tool that you can use or put aside.

Embracing the Possibility of Change

Adapting as You Learn:

This journey may change you. At first, you might feel a surge of excitement at each small victory: a waived fee here, an unauthorized upgrade there, a carefully extracted favor from someone who never suspects a thing. Over time, you may find yourself growing more comfortable testing the boundaries, or you might realize it's not worth the mental energy. Either way, this education empowers you. It shows you that many of life's obstacles are negotiable and that what you've been taught to accept can often be rearranged if you're daring enough.

Reflecting on the Big Picture:

As we close this chapter, think about the big picture. The world as you know it is a layered construct of rules, norms, and expectations. Most people glide through life accepting these structures as immovable. This book invites you to see them as flexible frameworks open to manipulation. Whether you end up using these skills frequently or sparingly, simply knowing they exist puts you in a different league. You're no longer the unwitting pawn; you're a player who understands how the game is played, and how it can be skewed.

Chapter 2:

Identifying "Gray Zones"

and Loopholes

Sometimes rules are strict, sometimes they're elastic, and often they're just poorly enforced. Even supposedly ironclad systems can reveal cracks through which a determined individual might slip. Chapter 1 introduced the idea that the world is built upon norms and regulations that many accept at face value, but once you open your eyes to the possibility of bending them, a whole spectrum of opportunities appears.

This chapter delves into those specific opportunity areas, "gray zones" of everyday life that are neither overtly legitimate nor flatly illegal. We'll discuss how to spot these weaknesses and interpret them in a way that benefits you. By the end of this chapter, you should be able to see beyond the veneer of bulletproof policies and realize that many rules have hidden seams and vulnerabilities ripe for exploitation.

Spotting Loopholes in Systems

The Nature of Loopholes

Loopholes aren't always the dramatic legal escapes you hear about in corporate or political scandals. Often, they're small oversights, vague lines in a policy, or poorly updated procedures that a watchful individual can leverage. A store's return policy might claim "full refund within 30 days," but fail to specify that the item must be unused. An airline might offer complimentary rebooking if your flight is delayed by more than an hour, but never define how they measure that delay. In each case, the system leaves a crack open for someone bold enough to walk through.

Why Loopholes Exist:

1. **Human Error and Oversight:** Most policies are written by committees more concerned with covering major risks than perfecting every detail.

2. **Rapid Change and Legacy Rules:** As companies evolve, merging, restructuring, or adopting new technology, old rules may remain on the books, unaligned with new practices.

3. **Customer Service Priorities:** Many organizations prioritize customer satisfaction over enforcement of small print. They'd rather lose a bit of money than antagonize a potentially loyal (or loudly complaining) patron.

When you encounter a policy or system, remember that it was designed by humans. Ask yourself: "What did the policy writers assume I would do?" Then consider how you can circumvent those assumptions. For instance, if a rewards club only checks membership numbers occasionally, might you repeatedly cash in on promotions that are intended to be single-use?

Mining Websites, Contracts, and Terms & Conditions

In modern life, many of the crucial "rules" we face appear online: digital contracts, terms and conditions pop-ups, user agreements for services, disclaimers on booking pages, etc. Most people click "Agree" without reading them, but if you scan for certain keywords, such as "except," "limited to," "may be subject to," "at our discretion", you'll often find openings.

- **Look for Exceptions:** Phrases like "in select circumstances" or "unless otherwise noted" can indicate potential escape clauses. If a policy states, "Refunds are issued only if the item is returned within 14 days, except in certain cases," you've found a wedge. Find out what "certain cases" might be.

- **Ambiguous Language:** Whenever a policy uses vague language like "reasonable," "adequate proof," or "satisfactory performance," you have a door to push. "Reasonable" to whom? "Adequate" by what metric? In these gray areas, your interpretation may clash with theirs, but you have room to argue your case.

Savvy travelers often exploit airline terms that mention "involuntary re-routing" or "overbooking situations." They keep an eye on flight loads or known delays, and when the right scenario arises, they request free changes or upgrades under that vague clause. The airline staff might balk, but if it's spelled out in the company's own documents, the traveler has a legitimate foot in the door.

Using Community Knowledge

In the age of social media and user forums, you're rarely the first person to notice a loophole. Reddit, Quora, dedicated Facebook groups, and niche Discord servers often serve as treasure troves of discovered hacks. Some may be outdated, while others might be brand new. If you're serious about finding everyday angles, monitor these digital spaces. People love to brag about how they got their money's worth or overcame a policy. By analyzing their methods, you can replicate or refine them for your own use.

- **Subreddits (reddit.com) like /r/Frugal, /r/PersonalFinance, or /r/Hacking** often include threads discussing system exploits, some ethical, some less so.

- **Product or Merchant-Specific Forums** can reveal known issues or vulnerabilities. For example, if a certain store's self-checkout machines are notoriously buggy, someone may share a method of scanning certain items twice and paying less.

Staying up to date is crucial. Companies and institutions often patch these holes once they become too well-known. By the time a hack hits mainstream news, it's probably dead. Your best bets lie in niche online communities, behind paywalls, or among small circles of friends who keep their secrets close.

Exploiting Ambiguity and "Fine Print"

The Power of Vague Language

In many cases, a policy's worst enemy is its own vagueness. If the fine print doesn't explicitly forbid a particular action, you can claim plausible innocence when you take advantage of it. For instance, a coupon might say "One per household," but never define what constitutes a household. Could your basement rental or guest suite qualify as a second "household"? If no further clarification is provided, you might argue that your sibling or roommate is a separate entity, doubling your redemption potential.

Similarly, loyalty programs might say "Employees and their immediate family are not eligible." But do they define "immediate family"? Does that exclude your second cousin or your best friend living with you? If not, you have a technical argument in your favor.

Exploiting Trials, Promotions, and Discounts

Free trials and promotional offers are often riddled with fine-print pitfalls, sometimes in your favor. Companies typically assume minimal abuse because many people don't have the patience to continually recreate accounts or juggle different email addresses. But if you're determined, you can exploit these cracks.

- **Multiple Email Accounts:** Create additional accounts using different email services. Yes, it's a cliché, but it remains effective. Many companies rely on email addresses as primary identification and do not cross-check further data like IP addresses or payment details.

- **Disposable Virtual Cards:** For services that require a payment method at sign-up, consider using virtual credit cards from fintech companies or banks that let you generate unique card numbers. This way, you can keep your real information separate and circumvent "one card per user" restrictions.

- **Stacking Promotions:** If a service or merchant doesn't explicitly prohibit combining offers, try applying multiple discount codes. You might discover that the system honors them in succession, drastically cutting your bill. When challenged, you can maintain you didn't realize there was a limit, after all, the system processed it without complaint.

A common example is meal kit subscriptions. Many new users sign up for a "first month 50% off" deal, then cancel. If they wait a few weeks and rejoin with a different email address (and sometimes a different payment method), they often qualify for a "welcome back" coupon. Rinse and repeat, and you'll rarely pay full price, unless or until the company notices a pattern and cracks down.

Policies with Undefined Consequences

Some returns policies or membership agreements talk about punishing abuses but never detail what that punishment entails. If you find yourself at odds with them, say, you made too many returns or exploited multiple promotions, ask, "What does that violation mean in practical terms? Are you going to fine me? Terminate my account?" If the policy never spelled it out, they might bluff. Corporations have "internal use only" guidelines on enforcement that they rarely share publicly. If you're persistent and knowledgeable, they might let you off with a warning, because legally they may not have the standing to do more.

Sizing Up Targets and Situations

Low-Hanging Fruit vs. High-Risk Targets

Not all loopholes are created equal, and not all targets are worth pursuing. If you're pushing a massive multinational retailer for a minor discount, the risk is low, they handle countless daily transactions and losing a few dollars to you barely registers. But if you're trying to exploit a local mom-and-pop shop, the moral and social consequences might be greater. You could face immediate confrontation, damage personal relationships, or gain a negative reputation in a tight-knit community.

Likewise, bigger hacks might yield bigger rewards but come with higher scrutiny. High-value targets, like banks, airlines, or government agencies, often have more robust security, data analytics, and legal teams. You'll need a smarter strategy and stronger nerves to exploit them successfully. It's easier to argue a $10 refund on a questionable transaction with a small business or an automated system than to, say, manipulate an insurance payout. The latter might land you on the radar of a fraud investigation unit if you're not careful.

Assessing Institutional Blind Spots

An effective unethical hacker, whether in cybersecurity or everyday life, knows how to identify blind spots. These blind spots arise when an institution invests resources in certain areas of compliance or security but neglects others. Examples:

1. **Front-Desk vs. Online Inconsistencies:** A hotel's online booking system might strictly control discount codes, while the front desk might have the leeway to adjust rates on the fly for disgruntled customers.

2. **Departmental Silos:** In large organizations, different departments often don't communicate perfectly. A billing department might not see a complaint resolved by customer service. By playing these silos against each other, you can sometimes secure extra credits or refunds.

3. **Overworked Employees:** Institutions heavily reliant on underpaid or overwhelmed staff are ripe for exploitation. When employees are juggling multiple tasks, they're less likely to verify every detail, especially if you appear confident and polite.

Timing Is Everything

Timing can be the difference between success and a firm "no." Approaching an employee at a busy hour might mean they don't have the bandwidth to challenge you; they just want to clear the queue. Conversely, if you catch someone at the end of their shift, they may want to finalize everything quickly. Some unethical opportunists even plan calls or visits close to closing time, knowing staff might cut corners to go home on time.

- **Corporate Fiscal Quarters:** Many companies are under pressure to meet financial metrics at the end of a quarter. That can mean they're more desperate to close deals, or more generous in appeasing customers if it means avoiding bad publicity that might hurt quarterly reports.

- **Off-Peak Seasons:** During slow seasons, businesses may bend rules to win or retain any customer interest they can. Negotiating a free hotel upgrade or service credit is often easier when demand is low.

Gauging Who Cares (and Who Doesn't)

One of the most important lessons in identifying and leveraging loopholes is understanding **who cares enough** to enforce the rule. If an employee personally benefits from ignoring a regulation, such as making a commission or avoiding a negative customer satisfaction score, they might look the other way. Conversely, if the person responsible for enforcing the rule is personally invested or under strict guidance from management, you can expect more pushback.

- **Example:** A customer service agent might have authority to issue $50 in credits without a manager's approval. Anything above $50 requires escalation. Target requests around that threshold so they can easily comply without hassle.

- **Example:** A small event organizer might be stricter about gatecrashers than a massive trade show with thousands of attendees. At the large event, checking every badge is impractical; at the small event, each attendee is more visible.

Bringing It All Together

Loopholes come in many shapes: ambiguous language, outdated policies, mislabeled goods, understaffed support lines, or system oversights. Your task is to learn to see what others miss, to test boundaries, and to interpret instructions in self-serving ways. This doesn't require genius, just attentiveness, creativity, and the confidence to push where others yield.

1. **Stay Informed:** Keep an eye on forums, online communities, and social media groups where people discuss deals, freebies, or system flaws.

2. **Research the Fine Print:** Scrutinize terms, conditions, and disclaimers. Highlight any vague or contradictory statements.

3. **Experiment Tactically:** Try small tests before going for a big win. If you suspect you can combine discount codes, attempt it with a low-cost purchase first.

4. **Use Polite Persistence:** If you're told "no," ask for a supervisor. If the supervisor isn't helpful, hang up and call again. Different reps interpret rules differently.

5. **Know When to Retreat:** Some loopholes won't be worth the risk or headache. If a target begins to push back aggressively, weigh the benefit of continuing versus walking away with minimal losses.

Extended Example: Gaming a Gym Membership

To illustrate these principles, let's consider a scenario involving a gym membership. Many gyms run introductory deals, "Join now for $1!", with the expectation that you'll commit to a year's contract at a monthly rate. The fine print might say you can cancel within 30 days if unsatisfied, but it might also contain contradictory language about certain fees.

- **Step 1: Read the Contract:** You notice that the contract states "no cancellation fee if canceled within 30 days," but it also says, "a $50 processing fee applies to cancellations." Are these fees the same? Possibly not. You could argue the "processing fee" is different from a "cancellation fee," and that you shouldn't be subject to both.

- **Step 2: Spot the Ambiguity:** Next, you see "Cancellation requests must be submitted in writing," but the contract doesn't explicitly define "in writing." Does email count? A text message? A letter with a postmark before the 30-day mark? If you submit an email on day 29, you could challenge them if they claim you missed the window.

- **Step 3: Exploit the Loophole:** You sign up for the $1 trial, enjoy the facilities for 29 days, then send an email to the manager stating you're canceling. If they attempt to charge the $50 processing fee, you reference the part of the contract that indicates "no cancellation fee." You push back: "Is that the same as a processing fee? Because it's not clearly stated. I'd be happy to escalate this." Often, rather than fight a lengthy dispute, they might simply cancel without charging additional fees.

- **Step 4: Bonus Round, Sign Up Again:** If the gym repeatedly runs promotions with no system in place to track old members, you could rejoin a few months later under a slight variation of your name or address, "A. Jackson" instead of "Andrew Jackson," for example. You exploit the lack of identity verification, repeatedly enjoying discounted trial periods as if you're a new customer each time.

This example underscores how everyday policies can be interpreted in multiple ways if the language is sloppy or the enforcement is lax. It doesn't matter that the gym "intended" the $50 processing fee to cover early termination; if they failed to clearly articulate that in the contract, you have leverage.

The Opportunist's Lens

Identifying gray zones and loopholes isn't about memorizing an endless list of specific hacks. It's about adopting a new way of seeing the world. Where others read rules and comply, you read rules and wonder, "Is there a different angle here?" Where others gloss over dense contract language, you scan it looking for cracks and contradictions. Where most people see a policy as rigid, you see a policy as a negotiation.

This shift in perspective forms the bedrock of the unethical approach outlined in this book. Once you fully internalize it, you'll find that countless everyday situations present minor (and sometimes major) chances to exploit ambiguities or to interpret guidelines in your favor. These opportunities are invisible to the average person precisely because they accept norms without question. You, however, will become the person who questions everything.

Yet, remember: simply identifying a loophole doesn't guarantee success. Execution matters. You'll need confidence, social finesse, and sometimes a willingness to endure friction if someone pushes back. That's where future chapters come in, exploring how to reduce risk, cover your tracks, and handle confrontations. But none of that matters without first learning to see the cracks. The world is full of them, if only you learn where and how to look.

In the next chapter, we'll dive deeper into minimizing personal risk and exposure, building on your new ability to spot loopholes. After all, what good is a cunning plan if you're caught in the act? We'll talk about strategies for maintaining plausible deniability, covering your digital footprints, and preparing a well-crafted story for when someone inevitably raises an eyebrow at your too-good-to-be-true advantage. Until then, keep your eyes open, gray zones are everywhere, waiting for you to exploit them.

Chapter 3:
Minimizing Personal Risk and Exposure

So, you've learned to spot cracks in the system, those lovely gray zones and loopholes that let you bend rules to your advantage. Now comes the practical question: **How do you use these tactics without getting caught?** After all, even the tiniest ethical infraction can become a big problem if you attract the wrong kind of attention. Perhaps a smirking manager decides to investigate, or a suspicious algorithm flags your repeated "new customer" sign-ups. Remaining unnoticed (or at least unchallenged) is the real art of the unethical life hack.

In this chapter, we'll dive into key strategies for protecting yourself from scrutiny. We'll explore how to maintain plausible deniability, how to shield your digital footprint, and how to orchestrate your questionable activities so they appear accidental or benign. By the time you turn to the next chapter, you should have a firm grasp on how to minimize both moral and legal repercussions for your cunning maneuvers.

Maintaining Plausible Deniability

The Power of Innocent Appearances

Plausible deniability means you can credibly claim ignorance or unintentional error if someone tries to corner you. If you're ever challenged, "Hey, didn't you notice you applied three discount codes at once?", your goal is to remain convincingly confused or well-intentioned. Adopt the wide-eyed sincerity of someone who believed they were just following normal procedure. If your usage of loopholes seems obviously deliberate, you'll be quickly labeled a cheat. But if you come across as a naive or benign participant, you might get off with a warning or no consequence at all.

1. **Feign Confusion:** Use phrases like, "I'm sorry, I just pressed the button and it worked," or "I must have misunderstood. I didn't realize I was only allowed one discount."

2. **Shift Responsibility:** If a staff member made a mistake on your behalf, such as applying an extra promo code, act as though you assumed it was part of the deal. "I just asked if there was a better price, and they gave it to me!"

3. **Document Everything (Selectively):** Sometimes you'll want an email or chat transcript showing a representative approved your questionable request. That way, if challenged later, you can say, "Customer service said it was fine!"

When to Play Dumb vs. When to Play Smart

Knowing which persona to adopt can be a fine art. If you're dealing with front-line employees who don't have deep system knowledge, acting confused can make them more likely to brush off your transgression. On the other hand, if you're speaking to a manager or an executive with authority, playing too dumb can raise suspicion. They might think, "Nobody can be that clueless." In such cases, a lightly informed approach can work wonders:

- **Lightly Informed:** "Yes, I read your policy about returns, and it said I just needed my receipt. Now you're telling me there's an extra step? Maybe I misread, but it really wasn't clear."

Striking the right balance shows you're neither an expert schemer nor a fool. You've done some homework but still rely on **their** guidance to clarify the fine points. This can be disarming because it frames your request as a simple misunderstanding rather than a blatant manipulation.

Building a Backstory

If a particular hack requires multiple steps, like creating multiple "new user" accounts, you should prepare a simple but believable backstory in case questions arise. For instance, if you're using multiple emails to exploit a streaming service's free trial:

1. **Different Identities:** "Oh, that's my family member's account. We share a computer. Are we not allowed to do that?"

2. **Household Chaos:** "My roommate and I both wanted to try the service. I didn't realize we were only allowed one trial per address."

3. **Occasional Lying by Omission:** Sometimes you won't need to fabricate details, just omit the relevant truth. If asked, you can say, "No, I don't remember creating another account. Maybe it auto-logged me in."

In each scenario, the objective is to look like someone who got tangled up in the rules rather than someone determinedly gaming the system.

Covering Your Digital Tracks

In an era of data analytics, algorithms, and digital footprints, your online behavior can be a dead giveaway if you're not careful. Many companies track IP addresses, payment methods, and usage patterns to spot unusual activity. If your goal is to exploit multiple free trials or bend e-commerce systems, **concealing your digital identity** is critical.

Using Alternate Email Addresses and Aliases

Multiple Email Providers

This is the most straightforward tactic: set up new accounts with different email addresses from Gmail, Yahoo, ProtonMail, or other providers. However, be aware that some companies now track patterns of similar usernames. If your main email is example@gmail.com, try not to create multiple addresses like example@protonmail.com. Instead, get creative:

- Example420@gmail.com

- Examp13@gmail.com

- 1_example6969@gmail.com

Sprinkle in random numbers or letters to avoid detection. Alternatively, use email forwarding services that let you create aliases instantly, funneling all messages to your main inbox.

Name Variations

When entering account details, use slight variations of your name. For instance, if your name is Jane Elizabeth Doe, you might create separate user profiles as:

- Jane E. Doe

- J. Elizabeth Doe

- J. E. Doe

As long as your payment method doesn't contradict the name, many systems won't notice. This subtle change can bypass certain duplicates-detection filters that rely on matching first and last names exactly.

Hiding Your IP Address

VPNs and Proxy Servers

A virtual private network (VPN) routes your internet traffic through a different location, masking your real IP address. If you're repeatedly signing up for free trials, a VPN can fool services that use IP addresses as an indicator of returning customers. Some streaming sites do crack down on known VPN servers, but many still allow them.

- **Rotate Locations:** Don't always pick the same server location. If you keep popping up in the same city, that data can become suspicious.

- **Paid VPNs vs. Free VPNs:** Free VPNs often come with limited server options and may leak data. Paid VPNs typically offer more reliable anonymity and more global server selections.

Using Mobile Data

If you have a smartphone data plan, you can switch between Wi-Fi and mobile data when creating new accounts. Many websites track your public IP address when you sign up; simply toggling off Wi-Fi can generate a new IP from your mobile provider, reducing the chance of immediate detection.

Disposable Virtual Credit Cards

One of the trickiest aspects of repeated sign-ups is the payment method. Some platforms require a valid credit card to verify identity. This is where disposable virtual cards come in handy. Services like Privacy.com or certain fintech apps let you generate a new card number for each transaction. Each card can have a spending limit or a "burn" date, preventing the merchant from charging you after the trial period (assuming you "forgot" to cancel).

- **Keep Track of Each Card:** If you create multiple virtual cards, label them in your app or spreadsheet so you don't mix them up.

- **Vary Billing Addresses:** Some virtual card providers allow you to set different billing addresses for each card. Use variations if the service you're signing up for cross-checks addresses.

Making the Scam Look Accidental

Not every exploit will appear purposeful. Sometimes your best shield is the illusion that you've simply stumbled into a beneficial glitch or been the lucky recipient of an unintended perk. This can be especially useful in face-to-face interactions with customer service, retail staff, or event organizers.

Playing the "Oops" Card

If you're called out for using multiple coupons, you might say, "Oh, I entered them both, and the system accepted it, I assumed it was allowed." That single statement shifts blame to the system, painting you as a passive beneficiary of a programming quirk rather than a schemer.

Acting Surprised, Not Guilty

The difference between "surprised" and "guilty" body language can be huge. If you're confronted:

- **Raise your eyebrows:** Indicate confusion or disbelief, not fear.

- **Maintain or slow your breathing:** Quickened breathing can signal anxiety, so keep it calm.

- **Avoid defensive or exaggerated gestures:** Shrug gently, nod attentively, but don't flail your arms.

This helps you appear less like a cornered criminal and more like someone baffled by a misunderstanding.

Leveraging Store or System Errors

Sometimes stores mislabel items, or websites display incorrect prices. If you notice a mislabeled product, you might buy it in bulk or challenge the cashier for a price match. Should a manager confront you, claim you're merely asking for the store to honor its displayed price (common policy in many regions). You're not demanding something unethical; you're just taking advantage of their error, a plausible stance in most consumer protection environments.

Handling Confrontations and "Near Misses"

Even with careful planning, you might encounter a gatekeeper who spots suspicious activity. Maybe an employee has seen the same coupon code from the same address too many times, or a manager notices the same ID being used for multiple returns. Knowing how to handle confrontations is crucial to minimizing fallout.

De-escalation Tactics

1. **Keep Your Cool:** Never panic. The moment you display fear, it becomes evident you have something to hide.

2. **Ask Questions:** Turn the tables gently. "What do you mean I'm not allowed? The promotion banner didn't say anything about a limit." This forces them to provide details, giving you potential wiggle room.

3. **Offer a Sincere Apology:** If pressed, a quick, straightforward apology can diffuse tension. "I'm so sorry, I really didn't realize. Let me fix that immediately." This often stops a situation from escalating further.

Redirecting Blame

Sometimes you can pin the oversight on a third party, a friend, a family member, or even a glitchy system:

- **"My partner set this up."** If they challenge your multiple sign-ups, claim your partner or roommate handles these things.

- **"I used the mobile app, and it auto applied the discount."** Feign ignorance about app functionality.

- **"I saw this on your website."** Even if it was a glitch, you can act like you trusted their official channel.

The goal here isn't to be morally pristine; it's to ensure the confrontation ends in a stalemate, or better yet, with you walking away unscathed.

Knowing When to Cut Losses

Sometimes, pushing back too hard can escalate the problem. If the manager or employee is determined to hold their ground, it may be safer to abandon this particular hack and walk away. Creating a public scene or drawing in higher-level staff might escalate what was once a low stakes exploit into a serious issue. A prudent rogue knows when to cut their losses: accept a single coupon, pay a small fee, or settle for a partial victory rather than risk being banned or flagged in the system.

Real-Life Scenarios of Low-Risk Tactics

To illustrate these concepts, let's look at a few hypothetical but plausible scenarios.

Scenario 1: Streaming Service Trials

- **The Tactic:** You plan to rotate free trials on a streaming platform by using multiple emails and virtual credit cards.

- **Minimizing Exposure:**

    o   Use a VPN to change your IP each time.

    o   Vary the names on each account (e.g., "John M. Smith," "Jonathan Smith," "J. M. Smith").

    o   If questioned, claim you have multiple roommates who all tried the service.

- **Accidental Appearance:**

    o   If ever confronted by customer service, say, "My family and I share devices, maybe it linked our accounts?"

o   Provide a credit card screenshot from your virtual card if needed, showing a legitimate transaction (the $0 hold).

Scenario 2: Hotel Upgrades

- **The Tactic:** Politely but persistently request an upgrade at check-in by citing a vague hotel policy that "Gold members get complimentary room upgrades when available."

- **Minimizing Exposure:**

  o   Appear to be a loyal customer by knowing some basics about the hotel chain's rewards program.

  o   If denied, calmly ask if there's any courtesy upgrade for special occasions or "loyal guests."

- **Accidental Appearance:**

  o   If the front desk clerk seems suspicious, play confused. "Oh, I read an article online saying this was standard for Gold members. Sorry if I misunderstood!"

  o   This frames your attempt as misguided enthusiasm rather than scheming.

Scenario 3: Returning Used Merchandise

- **The Tactic:** Purchase an item, use it briefly, then return it claiming you found a defect or that it "just didn't fit your needs."

- **Minimizing Exposure:**

  - o Keep packaging in good shape. Slightly re-box it as though it wasn't used heavily.

  - o Have a simple story about why it didn't work for you. ("It was the wrong size," "My spouse hated the color," etc.)

- **Accidental Appearance:**

  - o If a suspicious employee checks for wear and tear, say, "Oh, I only used it once for a test. I had no idea it would show wear so quickly, must be a quality issue."

  - o This positions you as disappointed in the product rather than exploiting the return policy.

Ethical Considerations and Psychological Consequences

While the focus here is on evading detection, let's address the elephant in the room: **guilt and long-term ramifications**. Even if you successfully avoid legal or financial trouble, repeated deception can take a psychological toll. Acting clueless or dishonest repeatedly may alter how you perceive yourself and how you interact with others.

- **Cognitive Dissonance:** You may feel uneasy reconciling your cunning activities with the self-image of being an honest person.

- **Normalization of Dishonesty:** The more often you manipulate systems, the more likely you are to see deception as your default approach, which can bleed over into personal relationships.

- **Reputational Damage:** If friends, colleagues, or family discover your underhanded tactics, they might lose trust in you.

No matter your stance on morality, it's worth considering these factors as part of your risk assessment. The best unethical hackers remain keenly aware of their own boundaries and the potential fallout on their relationships and peace of mind.

Summarizing Key Strategies

1. **Plausible Deniability:** Act as though you had no idea you were breaking a rule. Keep your requests or actions modest enough that they seem accidental.

2. **Digital Camouflage:** Employ alternate emails, aliases, VPNs, and virtual credit cards to avoid detection by automated systems.

3. **Accidental-Looking Exploits:** Always have an explanation that places blame on the system or your ignorance, not your intent.

4. **Confrontation Management:** If challenged, stay calm, ask polite questions, and apologize if necessary. Know when to bail out to avoid bigger problems.

5. **Psychological Boundaries:** Recognize your personal comfort zone. Be mindful of the mental and social repercussions of repeated deception.

The Art of Going Unnoticed

As you continue to delve into the world of unethical life hacks, remember that your greatest ally is the **appearance of legitimacy**. The best deceptions are the ones that never raise an eyebrow because they seem plausible, accidental, or too minor to warrant investigation. Whether you're claiming multiple discounts, returning used items, or stacking loyalty rewards, you'll find most corporations, vendors, and gatekeepers too preoccupied to chase small-scale transgressions, provided you don't wave a red flag.

Yet, an essential aspect of your journey is self-awareness. Continuously ask yourself if the payoff is worth the risk, both legally and emotionally. The stakes can range from a minor scolding all the way up to blacklisting or legal action, depending on how far you push and who you cross. Knowledge of how to dodge detection is power, but power can corrupt. Proceed with caution, weigh your decisions, and keep your moral compass (however flexible it may be) within reach.

Chapter 4:
Social Engineering and Subtle Manipulation

It's often said that life is a game of people, not rules. Policies and loopholes only get you so far if you lack the capacity to influence those who enforce, or overlook, them. This is where social engineering and subtle manipulation come into play. By reading personalities, planting ideas, and framing situations, you can persuade people to grant you favors or bend the rules without realizing they're being nudged.

Make no mistake: This chapter covers ethically murky territory. When you leverage the quirks of human behavior for personal gain, you enter a realm where success can hinge on empathy, deception, and moral flexibility in equal measure. Yet, social engineering doesn't always rely on unkind or nefarious tactics, sometimes, a well-placed compliment or a tailored request can achieve your aims without undue harm. Wherever you stand on the moral scale, these methods will expand your toolkit for navigating everyday interactions with cunning and confidence.

Reading People's Signals

The Foundation of Influence

Before you can manipulate someone, you need to understand what makes them tick. People telegraph their vulnerabilities, motivations, and biases through subtle cues, body language, tone of voice, choice of words, even the type of coffee they order. Successful social engineers are astute observers, constantly picking up on micro-expressions or emotional undercurrents that might reveal how to approach a target.

1. **Body Language Clues:** Watch for signs of stress (fidgeting, tight jaw, clenched fists), openness (relaxed shoulders, eye contact, palms visible), or hesitancy (crossed arms, avoiding eye contact, half-smiles).

2. **Emotional State:** Is the person rushed, bored, frustrated, or eager to please? Matching or gently altering that state can be a key to compliance.

3. **Contextual Factors:** Who's around? Are they in a public setting, at work, at a social gathering? Different contexts shift how readily a person will bend rules or grant favors.

For example, a security guard late in their shift might be more lenient if they're tired or eager to go home. A customer service representative in a bustling call center might be more willing to grant refunds if they're under pressure to move quickly. Recognizing these situational cues gives you an instant edge.

Identifying Personality Types That Are Easy to Influence

While it's dangerous to overgeneralize, certain personality traits correlate with higher susceptibility to manipulation:

- **People-Pleasers:** They hate conflict and love being liked. If your request appears friendly and non-threatening, they'll often comply to maintain harmony.

- **Naïve or Distracted Individuals:** If someone is new on the job or overworked, they might not think twice about a questionable request. They're too busy or inexperienced to scrutinize the details.

- **Ego-Driven Gatekeepers:** Counterintuitively, people with big egos can be easier to manipulate if you stroke their sense of importance. For instance, "I can tell you're really experienced, maybe you could help me figure out this issue?" This flattery can lower their guard.

Likewise, recognize when someone is not easily swayed, maybe they're highly trained, extremely detail-oriented, or personally invested in enforcing rules. Approach these gatekeepers with caution or try to circumvent them entirely.

Planting Ideas in Others' Minds

The Subtle Art of Suggestion

The most effective manipulation often feels like the other person's idea. If they believe they arrived at a conclusion independently, they'll rarely question its legitimacy. This is the principle behind "inception", slipping suggestions into someone's mind so smoothly that they adopt them as their own.

1. **Use Leading Questions:** Instead of saying, "Give me a discount," ask, "Is there any flexibility in the pricing for someone who's been a loyal customer?" By posing it as a question, you allow the other person to feel like they're the one offering the solution.

2. **Seed Desired Outcomes Early:** Let's say you want an event organizer to give you a VIP pass. Start by casually mentioning you've heard how VIP passes can sometimes be won or gifted, or how you noticed an extra pass lying around. You're planting the seed that giving you a pass isn't out of the ordinary, it's already "in the air."

3. **Reciprocity Hints:** Remind them, very gently, of something nice you've done in the past. "I remember helping you with your last-minute requests last year. Is there anything available this time around?" You're nudging them to even the karmic scale.

The Power of Flattery and Empathy

Humans are social creatures who crave validation. A well-timed compliment or demonstration of empathy lowers defenses.

- **Compliment Work Ethic:** If someone is working hard, acknowledge it: "I can see how busy you are, and you're handling it so smoothly! Could you possibly help me figure this out?"

- **Emotional Mirroring:** Reflect the other person's mood or concerns. "I know this policy can be stressful on your end; I really appreciate your help in resolving it."

When you combine praise with empathy, you're telling them, "I see you, I get you, and I value you." In that emotional comfort zone, people become more receptive to your requests.

Framing Requests and Situations

Presenting Your Gain as Their Relief or Benefit

One of the cornerstones of subtle manipulation is reframing your request so the other person believes it benefits them, or at least spares them a hassle. For instance, suppose you want an airline gate agent to let you board an earlier flight at no extra charge:

- **The Wrong Way:** "Hey, can you just switch me to that flight? I don't want to wait."

- **The Right Way:** "I noticed your later flight is fully booked, and I'm on it. If you move me to the earlier one, you'll free up a seat for someone else who might really need it. Would that help you manage the load better?"

Now you're not just requesting a favor; you're offering a solution that could reduce their problem, overcrowding. Even if that flight isn't oversold, they might not know or care. They see your angle as mutually beneficial, not self-serving.

Re-contextualizing a Request to Appear Harmless

Sometimes, you need to couch your request in a larger story or context that makes it sound more trivial than it is. If you're trying to get a restaurant to remove an item from your bill:

- **Include a Believable Anecdote:** "I've been bringing friends here for years because I adore this place. I was so embarrassed this time because I found a hair in my soup, just a tiny one, but it put them off. Any chance you could help me out on the bill so I can keep singing your praises?"

By turning your complaint into a story about loyalty and mild embarrassment, you reduce the request's perceived harshness. It's not just about free money; it's about making amends for a minor slip that threatened your ongoing patronage.

Leveraging Emotional States for Compliance

Exploiting Stress, Urgency, and Relief

A well-worn tactic in social engineering is capitalizing on heightened emotions. When people are stressed, rushed, or otherwise in an altered state of mind, they're more likely to say "yes" just to end the interaction.

- **Timing is Key:** If you see someone juggling tasks or dealing with a long line, approach them with an air of calm and confidence. The disparity between their stress and your composure can make them comply quickly to keep things moving.

- **Urgency Tactic:** Frame your request as time-sensitive: "I'm in a real bind; I have to make this event in 20 minutes. If you could do this for me, it'd be a lifesaver!"

People often respond to urgent pleas, if only to be the hero who rescued you.

Conversely, you can offer **relief**: "I know you must be sick of hearing complaints all day. Let me make this simple for you…" By acknowledging their difficult situation and proposing an easy out, you set yourself up as a cooperative ally rather than a demanding nuisance.

Using Guilt Trips (Carefully)

Guilt can be a powerful motivator, but it's also risky. Overplay your hand, and you'll come across as manipulative. The art of guilt-tripping lies in subtlety:

- **Soft Guilt:** "You've always been so understanding before. I'd hate to think I can't rely on that now. Is there any way you can help me out?"

- **Societal Responsibility:** "I feel like a big company like yours probably has some leeway to help honest customers, especially in tough times like these."

These statements gently insinuate that the person (or their employer) would be callous not to help. But keep it mild, if they sense they're being strong-armed, they'll likely dig in their heels.

The Fine Line Between Influence and Bullying

Recognizing When You're Pushing Too Hard

While manipulation can yield results, it can also backfire if you cross into bullying, intimidation, or overt deception that leaves the other person feeling duped. Manipulation done poorly can damage your reputation or escalate into a confrontation. Watch for signs of resistance:

- **Increased Defensiveness:** If the person starts crossing their arms, avoiding eye contact, or speaking curtly, they might sense your angle.

- **Requests for Evidence or Explanation:** "Where exactly did you read that policy? Can I see the manager?" This indicates they're not simply wavering; they want proof.

- **Clipped Responses:** "I don't think that's possible." "We don't do that here." "You're mistaken." Once they get blunt, you know your subtle charms haven't worked.

At this point, you can pivot. Apologize or soften your approach. Sometimes, retreating gracefully is the best move, preserving the option to try again with a different angle, or a different person, later.

The "Polite Demand" Trap

In pursuit of compliance, you might lean too heavily on politeness. While it sounds counterintuitive, some people see unwavering niceness as suspicious, especially if your request is significant. Overly sweet talk can sound forced. Instead:

- **Mirror Their Energy:** If they're businesslike, keep your tone professional yet warm. If they're casual, slip into more relaxed speech.

- **Use Genuine Specifics:** Compliments land better when they're specific. Instead of "You're doing a great job," try "I really appreciate how quickly you've answered my questions so far."

Authenticity, even if partially staged, helps your subtle manipulations feel less contrived.

Real-World Examples of Social Engineering

Example 1: Upgrading at a Car Rental Counter

Scenario: You've booked the cheapest compact car to save money, but you really want an SUV without paying extra.

1. **Observing the Agent:** You notice the rental desk agent is a bit bored, flipping through screens.

2. **Building Rapport:** "Long day, huh? I bet it's been hectic. Thanks for handling everything so efficiently."

3. **Seeding the Idea:** "I loved the SUV I drove last time, I felt so much safer on these roads. But I couldn't swing the upgrade this trip unless there's some special you can offer…"

4. **Playing on Empathy or Ego:** "I'm sure you know more about these promotions than I do. Is there any courtesy upgrade available for frequent renters?"

5. **Outcome:** If they bite, they feel like the hero who found a special deal for a grateful customer. If they balk, you can shrug it off as a misunderstanding.

Example 2: Early Check-In at a Hotel

Scenario: You arrive several hours before standard check-in time, exhausted from a red-eye flight.

1. **Reading the Desk Clerk:** Are they swamped with guests or relatively free to handle your situation?

2. **Framing the Request:** "I'm so sorry to bother you, I came in on an overnight flight, and I'm wiped out. I'd be eternally grateful if there's a clean room available early."

3. **Suggesting Mutual Benefit:** "If I get my room now, that's one less person waiting later when it gets busy. It might help keep your lobby clear."

4. **Employing Vulnerability:** Let them see your tired state, slightly droopy eyes, yawns. People often respond to physical cues of exhaustion with sympathy.

5. **Outcome:** If the room is available, they're more likely to grant early check-in. If not, you haven't lost anything but a few polite words.

Example 3: Gaining Access to a Restricted Event

Scenario: There's a VIP-only after-party you want to enter, but your pass doesn't qualify.

1. **Observing the Gatekeeper:** Is it a strict professional security guard, or a casually dressed intern handling check-ins?

2. **Building Familiarity:** "Hey, I was here last year. I think you guys run a fantastic event, loved how smoothly everything went!"

3. **Planting Doubt About Rules:** "I saw online that some attendees with general admission could also check out the after-party if there was space. Is that not right?"

4. **Hinting at Reciprocity:** "I can give a great shout-out on social media and help promote the event if I get a chance to mingle inside."

5. **Outcome:** A less experienced gatekeeper might let you in, especially if they're uncertain about strict rules or crave positive feedback.

Ethical (and Personal) Ramifications of Social Manipulation

We'd be remiss not to consider the **ethical and psychological toll** of manipulating others regularly:

- **Erosion of Authentic Relationships:** If you habitually deceive or nudge people for personal gain, you might find it harder to form genuine connections.

- **Cognitive Dissonance and Guilt:** Selling half-truths can conflict with your self-image, creating stress or a gnawing sense of unease.

- **Reputation Damage:** If a manipulation is exposed, your reputation could suffer in your community or workplace. People rarely forgive or forget feeling used.

On the other hand, social engineering skills can be harnessed for more benign goals, like negotiating for fair treatment or championing causes that benefit you and others. The line between cunning persuasion and constructive advocacy can be thin, and it's up to you to decide where you stand.

Combining Social Engineering with Other Hacks

The greatest conquests often merge social engineering with the loophole spotting you learned in previous chapters. For instance, if you find a policy gap that might let you secure a double refund, you could amplify your odds by sweet-talking a customer service rep into approving your claim without a thorough review. Or, if you want to capitalize on a store's under-advertised promotion, you might convince a manager that your case meets the criteria, even if it technically doesn't, by confidently describing the policy in your own terms.

Remember, your manipulative abilities serve as the **human** element that technological or policy-based hacks often lack. A loophole might exist, but without the right social finesse, you might not pull it off. Conversely, a great manipulator can sometimes sway people even when no official loophole exists, simply by crafting a compelling narrative.

Key Takeaways

1. **Read the Room:** Mastering the art of subtle manipulation begins with understanding the emotional state, motivations, and personality of your target.

2. **Plant Ideas Carefully:** Guide people toward believing a solution was their own thought. Use gentle hints, leading questions, and heartfelt compliments.

3. **Reframe to Mutual Benefit:** When asking for a favor or a rule-bend, present it as if granting your request helps them, too. This lowers their resistance.

4. **Respect the Limits (Or Know When to Fold):** Bullying or overt lying can damage your reputation and escalate conflicts. Use tact, empathy, and soft guilt, then back off if you sense pushback.

5. **Ethical Balancing Act:** Recognize the potential harm you can cause. Think about your relationships, emotional well-being, and the possibility of being exposed.

By refining your ability to influence people without raising red flags, you'll discover that many rules and boundaries depend heavily on the human factor for enforcement. If you can charm, persuade, and empathize your way through an obstacle, you might not even need to resort to overt deceptions or policy exploits. In short, social engineering serves as the perfect complement to your arsenal of unethical life hacks, one that can open doors, smooth over hiccups, and cloak your actions in harmless goodwill.

Chapter 5:
Gaining Small Financial Advantages

Most of us deal with mundane financial transactions every single day, from swiping a card at the grocery store to paying our monthly utility bills. And in each of these interactions, there's almost always a hidden angle or opportunity to shave off a few dollars or snag an extra perk, if you know where to look. This chapter dives into those small (yet cumulatively significant) exploits that can help you save money or even turn a profit with minimal effort or risk. Think of it as a gentle dance between consumer savvy and ethical flexibility: You're not stealing, exactly, but you're certainly not playing by the rules everyone else blindly accepts.

By the end, you'll have an expanded toolkit for everyday life, from the way you handle retail store policies to the subtler manipulations of financial institutions. Some hacks are low-stakes and fairly benign, like stacking multiple coupons that "shouldn't" stack. Others graze closer to the edge of legality, exploiting bank policies or online billing systems that overlook minor discrepancies. Only you can decide how far you're willing to go. But regardless of your personal moral boundaries, the knowledge in this chapter will illuminate just how many small cracks there are in everyday financial systems.

Freebies and Samples, Exceeding the Limit

The Psychology of "One Per Customer"

Businesses love to advertise freebies: free appetizers, free product samples, or promotional giveaways labeled with "Limit one per customer." Most folks shrug and obey. But from a financial standpoint, "one per customer" is rarely enforced to the letter. Companies rely on social norms to keep people in line. They expect the average shopper to comply without fuss. However, if you're comfortable pushing boundaries, especially in larger retailers or online forums, you can often double or triple your freebies with minimal risk.

1. **Multiple Email Addresses and Accounts:** As touched on in earlier chapters, one of the simplest ways to secure multiple freebies is by using alternate emails or social media accounts. If you're dealing with a giveaway that requires you to sign up on a website, do so with different addresses, or have household members "help" by signing up.

2. **Alternate Pickup Methods:** In physical stores, consider returning on another day or visiting a different branch. If a sample station is manned by a rotating staff, they might not notice you came in before.

3. **Communication Gaps:** The person handing out samples at the front might not communicate with the person in

the back. You could grab a sample in one aisle, then slip over to the produce section's free tasting session.

Ethical Gray Area: You're not exactly robbing the store, but you're exceeding a courtesy that the business extended. How far you take this depends on how comfortable you are with turning a small goodwill gesture into a personal loophole exploit.

"Abuse with a Smile"

When you exploit freebies, a little charm goes a long way. Ask kindly for an extra sample "for your friend" or because you're "really curious about the flavor." Many employees, especially if they're paid hourly and not personally invested in the store's bottom line, will shrug and oblige. Don't appear furtive or greedy; act like it's the most natural request in the world.

- **Case Study: Free Coffee Refills**
  Some coffee shops have unclear refill policies, maybe you only get free refills if you're staying in the café, or if you bought a certain size. But if you approach the counter with a smile and say something like, "Hey, I'd love a quick warm-up of coffee, please," there's a solid chance they'll pour it without charging. They might assume you're a paying customer from earlier, or they simply don't care enough to question you.

The trick is to exude casual confidence. If they do push back, "I'm sorry, refills aren't free", feign surprise. "Oh, I thought they were. No worries!" You can either pay the extra or drop it, knowing you'll likely find success elsewhere or on another day.

Coupon Stacking and Promo Code Hustles

The Basics of Couponing

Every year, companies spend billions issuing coupons, digital and paper, to entice new customers or retain existing ones. They rely on the assumption that most people won't combine deals in ways that gut their profit margins. But coupon stacking is a simple, powerful way to get massive discounts.

1. **Digital vs. Paper Coupons:** Some retailers allow using one digital coupon (like a store app discount) and one paper manufacturer coupon on the same item. This is often buried in the fine print, but rarely enforced rigorously.

2. **Competitor Coupon Acceptance:** Certain stores accept competitors' coupons. If you find a store brand coupon from a rival supermarket, you might be able to use it at your local chain. People frequently forget this perk, allowing you to appear knowledgeable while playing dumb: "Oh, I thought you guys matched competitors?"

3. **Multiple Transactions:** Instead of trying to stack too many coupons in one transaction, split purchases into multiple smaller ones. Cashiers often assume you're just methodically following some extreme couponing strategy.

Important Note: Some cashiers are trained to watch for extreme stacking. If you sense hesitation, shift to a different register, come back during a busier time, or claim confusion: "Oh, I didn't know these couldn't be combined. Should we separate the transactions?" This frames you as a slightly misguided but well-intentioned shopper.

Promo Code Revelations

Online shopping yields even more opportunities. Many e-commerce platforms have outdated or overlapping promo codes. For instance:

- **Reusable Welcome Discounts:** Often, a "Welcome10" promo code for 10% off is meant for new customers only, but the system might not actually check if you're truly new. Create a fresh account, enter the code, and enjoy the discount repeatedly.

- **Stacking Multiple Codes:** Some websites unintentionally allow you to apply multiple codes in the same order. Try a sitewide discount plus a free shipping code, plus a holiday coupon. If the system accepts them, that's on them. If questioned, claim ignorance, "I just typed them in, and it worked."

- **Referral Loopholes:** Plenty of companies offer referral bonuses, like $10 off your next purchase for each friend you refer. Create "friend" accounts for yourself, or have a close circle exchanging referrals among one another. If the platform lacks robust identity checks, you can accumulate enough credits to cover entire orders.

Good to Know: Some websites attempt to patch these exploits quickly. If you discover a working stack or code glitch, use it while you can, but don't broadcast it on social media unless you're ready to see it shut down fast. Also, keep screenshots or order confirmations. If the retailer tries to rescind discounts later, you have proof that their system authorized it.

Banking and Billing "Oversights"

Moving from everyday retail into the realm of banking and monthly bills raises the stakes. While it's still possible to exploit oversight and policy gaps here, tread carefully: financial institutions often have better detection algorithms and stricter enforcement. That said, minor billing errors and overlooked fees can still be great sources of small advantages.

Negotiating Fees You "Actually Owe"

Many consumers believe bank fees are untouchable. Overdraft charges, annual credit card fees, late payment penalties, aren't they set in stone? Not necessarily.

- **Polite Persistence:** Call customer service and express mild distress: "I noticed this $35 overdraft fee. It's really tough on my budget. Is there any chance you could waive it, just this once?" In many cases, the bank will comply, especially if you're polite and maintain a decent account history.

- **Multiple Attempts:** If the first rep says "no," try again another time. Different agents have different thresholds for waiving fees. Some can authorize a one-time courtesy removal.

- **Chronic Complainer Strategy:** If you rack up multiple fees, you can space out your calls and complaints, playing the "I'm a loyal customer, but I'm so upset" card each time. Banks are wary of losing customers, so they might wave off a few fees to keep you pacified.

While this approach isn't a brazen exploit, it's a prime example of leveraging human discretion in large financial entities. If you do it sparingly and convincingly, you can dodge fees that most people just accept.

Timing Payments and Cancellations

Companies that bill monthly, utilities, streaming services, gyms, often have fuzzy grace periods or cycles. By understanding their billing cycles and utilizing carefully timed cancellations or late payments, you can slip in an extra week or two of service without being charged.

1. **Prorated or Postpaid Services:** If a gym only charges you at the end of each month, cancel right after the billing date to use the facilities for almost a full extra month before your membership formally ends.

2. **Credit Card Statements:** If a card issuer doesn't penalize you for partial late payments until after a certain number of days, you can effectively borrow money interest-free

for that window. Just be sure to pay before the penalty date hits.

3. **Trial Extensions via Cancellation:** Many online services automatically extend a trial when you hit the "cancel" button to entice you to stay. So if you're on Day 29 of a 30-day trial, click "cancel," and they might offer another free month.

Risk Factor: Repeatedly pushing your luck with late payments can ding your credit or lead to extra fees if you slip up. Know the difference between a mild oversight by the system and a consistent pattern that a company might eventually crack down on.

Practical Examples of Small Financial Exploits

Example 1: Exploiting Grocery Store Return Policies

Scenario: Some grocery chains, like Costco or Kroger, have generous return policies for items that don't meet quality standards. If you're truly unscrupulous, you might:

1. **Buy Bulk for a Party:** Purchase multiple boxes of pre-made appetizers or other expensive items.

2. **Claim Dissatisfaction:** Return the unopened boxes after the party, saying you found them "bland" or "unfresh."

3. **Outcome:** You effectively hosted a party on the store's dime.

While this is ethically dubious (you're lying about the product quality), it's a known exploit that some customers abuse, and employees are often compelled by company policy to process refunds without a fuss.

Example 2: Bank ATM Fee Reversals

Scenario: You consistently use out-of-network ATMs, incurring fees. Every couple of months, you call your bank and lament the fees you've been charged, citing travel or lack of local branches.

1. **Play the Loyal Customer:** "I've been with you for years; it's frustrating that I can't find a local ATM near my workplace. Could you possibly refund some of these fees?"

2. **Escalate if Denied:** Ask politely if a supervisor might have the discretion to waive them. Some banks allot each agent a monthly or quarterly budget for fee reversals.

3. **Outcome:** While you might not recoup every dollar, many banks will refund a portion or all of the fees, especially if you're mild and apologetic rather than demanding.

Example 3: Overlapping Shipping Offers

Scenario: An online retailer offers free express shipping if you sign up for their store credit card, plus a 15% off code for first-time customers, plus a sitewide "Buy One, Get One 50% Off" promotion.

1. **Create a Fresh Account:** Use a new email for the first-time customer discount.

2. **Apply for the Store Card:** You might get approved instantly, granting you free express shipping.

3. **Combine Sitewide Promo:** Add items to your cart that qualify for BOGO deals.

4. **Outcome:** End up paying a fraction of the original cost. If the retailer's website and checkout system don't prohibit stacking, you've done nothing "technically" wrong. You've merely accepted every available offer.

Weighing the Risks of Small-Scale Cheating

Potential Backlash and Ban

Small-scale financial hacks rarely draw major legal repercussions, especially if the sum of money is minor. However, companies have the right to ban or block customers who show suspicious patterns. A retailer could blacklist your email, refuse to honor future returns, or flag your account for manual review.

- **Online Platforms:** Amazon, for example, tracks return rates and behavior. If you abuse returns excessively, you risk an account shutdown.

- **Banking Institutions:** If a bank suspects intentional abuse, like opening multiple accounts to dodge fees or exploit sign-up bonuses, they can close your accounts, which may harm your banking history.

The Slippery Slope of Normalizing Deception

Every time you get away with a small financial hack, you might feel a rush of satisfaction, a confirmation that bending the rules is easy. But repeated successes can embolden you to try riskier tactics or become complacent about covering your tracks.

- **Ethical Fatigue:** You might justify bigger deceptions since "everyone else is doing it" or "companies have so much money." Eventually, you might slip into outright fraud, crossing a line that can have serious consequences.

- **Diminishing Returns:** Some hacks require time and mental energy, like juggling multiple email addresses or battling customer service lines. The incremental savings might not always be worth the hassle, so choose your battles wisely.

Strategies for Longevity and Low-Profile Gains

1. Rotate Targets: Instead of hammering one retailer or bank repeatedly, spread out your exploits. Use different stores' lenient return policies rather than abusing a single one. This reduces the odds that a particular institution will zero in on you.

2. Pace Yourself: If you discover a profitable exploit, like a glitch in an online store's promo code system, don't place ten orders in one day. Space them out over weeks or months, maintaining the illusion that you're just a normal customer who occasionally shops.

3. Keep Records: It might sound paradoxical, but track your hacks, including dates, order numbers, promo codes used, and any relevant terms and conditions you rely on. This documentation helps if you need to reference a policy or previous conversation. It also prevents you from accidentally reusing the same code or approach too often in too short a time.

4. Change Identities Carefully: If you're using multiple names, credit cards, or addresses, ensure you have a clean system to avoid mixing them up. A single slip, like giving the wrong billing address for the wrong credit card, can reveal the ruse.

Final Thoughts on Financial Exploits

At the heart of these small financial hacks is a simple truth: modern commerce is built on assumptions of honesty and compliance. When those assumptions meet cunning opportunism, the system often doesn't have enough deterrents or checks in place to counter every minor exploit. Whether it's as innocuous as snagging a second free sample at the grocery store or as brazen as hosting an entire event on a "return policy," the core principle remains the same, there's a gap between how a transaction is meant to work and how it can be twisted to your advantage.

Is it victimless?

In many cases, the cost is diffused. Large corporations have massive margins. However, small businesses might feel the sting more acutely, so weigh your conscience and the potential backlash. The more public and local the environment, the higher the social or reputational risk if you're caught out. If your moral boundaries are flexible enough to incorporate such methods, at least do a cost-benefit analysis: Are you saving pennies or genuinely making your life easier without incurring disproportionate risk?

Is it sustainable?

Over time, systems evolve. Retailers update policies, websites fix promo code glitches, banks refine detection algorithms. No single hack will last forever. The cunning trickster is always learning, adapting, and staying one step ahead of patches and policy changes. In that sense, consider these financial exploits as a continuous game of cat-and-mouse, a game you can keep playing so long as you remain vigilant, creative, and discreet.

Key Takeaways

1. **Everyday Financial Systems Have Gaps:** From "one per customer" freebies to coupon stacking and bank fee waivers, the consumer landscape is riddled with small opportunities.

2. **Focus on Smaller, Repeated Gains:** Many of these tactics revolve around modest but repeatable wins, 5% here, $10 there, an extra free trial, a waived membership fee. Over time, these add up.

3. **Watch for Overuse:** Abusing a single policy or platform can get you flagged or banned. Spread out your efforts and rotate strategies.

4. **Ethical and Reputational Risks:** Each exploit nudges you further along a gray moral gradient. Smaller financial hacks tend to remain low-risk, but carelessness can escalate trouble or harm local businesses.

5. **Adapt to Change:** Companies regularly update systems and patch holes. Stay current on emerging deals, policy changes, and new promo offerings to keep your advantage.

Chapter 6:

Gaming Work and

Professional Systems

Imagine yourself walking into the office on a typical Monday morning. Cubicles hum with fluorescent light and idle chatter. Emails roll in, meetings clutter calendars, and your to-do list grows by the minute. Now, consider that for many people, this daily routine represents a hierarchical system as rigid as any retail policy. At the same time, it's loaded with potential loopholes, vast grey zones in accountability, performance metrics, expense reporting, and more. Unlike a one-time coupon hustle, however, manipulating your workplace can have deeper ripple effects: promotions, raises, or the risk of termination if you're caught out.

This chapter addresses ways to bend or exploit the professional environment to your advantage, while minimizing exposure. We'll start with how to appear more productive without slaving away, then move to subtle manipulations of company policies and perks. Finally, we'll look at networking for personal gain, extracting resources, favoritism, and invisible boosts from colleagues, vendors, and even clients. By the end, you'll see how the cunning can thrive in corporate spaces that reward not just merit, but showmanship and backstage maneuvering.

Appear Productive Without Extra Effort

The Illusion of Busyness

In most workplaces, perception often matters as much as, if not more than, reality. Your bosses and coworkers see the veneer of your work: how frequently you send emails, how often you chime in during meetings, whether you stay late or come in early. By carefully curating these signals, you can craft a narrative of an ultra-productive employee, even if you're coasting on minimal real output.

1. **Email Timing:**

   - **Send or Schedule Emails at Odd Hours**: A widely circulated trick is to schedule your emails late at night or very early in the morning. Many email clients (like Outlook or Gmail) let you compose a message and send it later. When your boss sees you "working" at 6:00 a.m., they often assume you're motivated and dedicated.

   - **Respond Quickly to High-Level Requests**: Even if you're slacking elsewhere, jump on emails from executives or key decision-makers. A near-instant reply signals attentiveness and speeds their perception of your reliability.

2. **Manage Visibility in Meetings:**

- o **Strategic Speaking**: Avoid waffling. Prepare a quick, relevant point to speak up in each meeting, ideally early on. Appearing engaged from the outset can reduce scrutiny for the rest of the session.

- o **Summaries and Recaps**: If you can't contribute substantively, volunteer to send out meeting minutes or action items. People remember you as the "helpful" one, even if you're simply transcribing what others said.

3. **Parked Window Dressing**:

- o **Leaving a Jacket on Your Chair**: The old trick of leaving a personal item (jacket, bag, open laptop) at your desk creates the impression you're merely "stepped away" rather than gone for a leisurely lunch or a personal errand.

- o **Virtual Presence**: In remote settings, log into messaging platforms early. Set your status as "Available," then vanish if you want some downtime. Periodically move the mouse or send a quick chat response so it seems you're never truly offline.

Why It Works: People, especially managers, often lack the bandwidth to measure real productivity. They rely on superficial cues: Are you visible? Are you responsive? Do you speak up in meetings? Mastering these illusions can get you labeled a star performer with surprisingly little effort on actual tasks.

Exploiting Key Metrics and Busywork

Every workplace has Key Performance Indicators (KPIs) or some measure of productivity. These can be manipulated if you know what your team or manager values:

- **Focus on the Measurable:** If your KPI is the number of support tickets closed, learn to pick off the easiest, fastest-to-solve tickets. Let other staff handle more complex or time-consuming cases. Your "tickets closed" metric might soar, while your actual workload remains moderate.

- **Dramatic Show-and-Tell:** Showcase small victories in a big way. If you automate a 5-minute repetitive task, write up a short explanation to your team describing how you "improved efficiency by 200%." Most people won't dissect the actual time savings.

Caution: If your manipulations affect your coworkers (for instance, dumping tough tasks on them), you could breed resentment. You're gambling on management's limited oversight. Overplay your hand, and you might become the office pariah.

Bending Company Policies to Your Advantage

Navigating Vague PTO Rules

Paid Time Off (PTO) rules vary. Some companies track hours meticulously, others are famously lax, and a growing number even offer "unlimited" PTO. Regardless of the policy, subtle manipulations can expand your off-the-clock time.

1. **Incremental Extensions**:

    o   **Late Returns and Early Departures**: If you take a Monday off, consider quietly leaving early on the preceding Friday or "arriving late" the following Tuesday. Many managers won't deduct additional PTO if you frame it as minor schedule adjustments, especially if you maintain the "I'll check emails from home" façade.

    o   **Partial-Shift Ambiguity**: Some companies count half-day increments. If your policy isn't super strict, claim a half day on paper when you're really absent most of the day. As long as your tasks don't slip, you might skate by unnoticed.

2. **Unlimited PTO Exploits**:

    o   **Under the Radar**: In a company with unlimited PTO, ironically, people often take fewer days off because they fear looking lazy. You can flip this by taking more time off while maintaining the illusions of constant online presence (chapter 6.1 tactics).

    o   **Leveraging Trust**: If your manager rarely questions your whereabouts, you can pepper extended weekends or occasional mental health breaks throughout the year. The key is to deliver just enough visible work so no one checks the fine print.

Why This Matters: Time is money, and more importantly, it's your life. If your workplace policies are vague or reliant on an honor system, a careful approach can net you substantial personal freedom with minimal professional risk.

Expense Accounts and Corporate Cards

If your job includes client dinners, travel expenses, or a company credit card, there's ample room for "creative" usage, provided you don't raise obvious red flags.

- **Overlapping Personal and Professional Costs:**

  o **Combining Trips**: If you're traveling for work, extend your stay for personal leisure. Charge part of the hotel costs or meals under "travel days" or "post-meeting dinners." This works especially well if your department only requires summarized receipts.

  o **Subtle Upgrades**: Book an economy flight but pay a small difference for a seat upgrade out of your pocket, then expense the base fare. If your manager sees "Economy Class" on the invoice, they'll assume you're being frugal. Meanwhile, you've effectively gotten a discount on better service.

- **Disguising Extraneous Purchases**:

  o **Vague Expense Descriptions**: If your company doesn't demand itemized receipts for smaller purchases, you could blend a few personal items under "office supplies" or "client gifts." This is riskier, as some accounting departments do random audits.

  o **Rounding and Bundling**: When restaurants lump multiple items into a single line item like "Food and Beverages," it's easier to slip in personal drinks or add-ons. If the total doesn't look excessive, finance departments often waive it through.

Warning: Messing with expense accounts can lead to serious consequences if caught, up to and including termination or legal action. Keep it small and plausible. The more frequently and brazenly you do it, the higher the risk of an internal audit or coworker complaints.

Networking for Non-Legitimate Gains

Extracting Free Resources from Colleagues and Vendors

The business world thrives on reciprocal relationships. You do a favor for a coworker, and later they return the favor in kind. While that's normal office culture, you can push it further into exploitative territory:

1. **Colleague Expertise**:

   o **Pretend Helplessness**: If you have tasks that are tedious or difficult, occasionally feign confusion to prompt a more knowledgeable coworker into taking over. "I tried everything, but I'm stuck, mind showing me how you'd do it?" Some colleagues love demonstrating expertise, effectively taking work off your plate.

   o **Small Bribes**: Offer intangible "bribes" like praise in group chats or mention them positively to a supervisor. This social capital can coax them to do more for you next time.

2. **Vendor and Supplier Relationships**:

   o **Under-the-Table Discounts**: If you manage vendor relationships, you might hint that awarding the vendor an extended contract could hinge on special "incentives" or freebies, anything from gift cards to personal "samples." While clearly unethical and sometimes illegal (bribery territory), it happens in many industries.

   o **Vendor Swag Overload**: Vendors frequently shower clients with branded swag: shirts, mugs, or even gadgets. Nothing stops you from stockpiling or subtly requesting more than is "intended." You can re-gift or use these items for personal benefit with zero cost.

Ethical Pitfalls: These tactics can stray into outright corruption if you're exchanging company contracts for personal gain. Even if you remain within plausible deniability, your reputation could suffer if coworkers suspect you're siphoning resources.

Trading Favors That Are Hard to Refuse

In some workplaces, the currency of advancement is not cash, but favors, introductions, and recommendations. You can create a subtle IOU economy by doing "kindnesses" that position people to feel indebted:

- **Praised Introductions**: Offer to introduce a coworker to a higher-up or an influential contact. Once they benefit from this connection, be it a new project or a rung on the career ladder, you can later remind them of the favor when you need a champion or ally.

- **Covering Mistakes**: If you catch a colleague making an error that could land them in hot water, fix it quietly and let them know afterward. You've spared them embarrassment or reprimand, and they owe you. This kind of "secret rescue" fosters a sense of gratitude (and mild vulnerability) that you can leverage.

Threat vs. Charm: Avoid crossing into blackmail territory. Rather than threatening to expose an error unless they comply, emphasize your helpfulness: "I didn't want you to get in trouble, so I just fixed it. Let me know if I can ever count on you for a favor, too." That keeps the transaction cordial, not coercive.

Managing Reputation and Risk

The Curtain of Polite Deniability

Workplaces can be rife with gossip. One ill-timed slip of the tongue or suspicious expense report can damage your standing with colleagues or management. To sustain your manipulations:

1. **Keep a Low Profile with Your Exploits:**

   o **Compartmentalize:** Don't brag openly about your free upgrades or cunning time-off ploys. The more you share, the more likely it is that word spreads.

   o **Use Ambiguity:** If someone sees you stepping out of the office early, mention you have a "doctor's appointment," but remain vague. If they poke further, respond with a politely evasive "Personal matter." People are less likely to probe.

2. **Strategic Confession:**

   o **Fake Transparency:** Occasionally highlight a small, harmless "scam" you used for the company's benefit. "Hey, I negotiated a slightly better supplier rate by sweet-talking them." This fosters an aura of "I'm a resourceful go-getter who might bend the rules for the team," diverting suspicion from bigger manipulations that purely benefit you.

Aligning Allies, Dodging Foes

- **Identify Potential Whistleblowers**: Some coworkers might be moral absolutists or resentful enough to rat you out. Keep your distance or placate them if needed.

- **Build Strategic Alliances**: If your boss likes results and isn't too fussed about how you get them, cultivate that relationship. They might defend your quirks if they think you're a high performer. Alternatively, partner up with peers who also bend the rules, creating an unspoken pact of "you cover my back, I cover yours."

When to Pull Back: The workplace is a repeating ecosystem. Unlike a one-time store exploit, you'll see these people daily or weekly. If you push a scheme too far, say, repeatedly charging personal dinners to the company card, someone will likely notice patterns. Weigh the short-term gain against the long-term career damage.

Real-World Examples of Professional Exploits

Example 1: Inflating Billable Hours in Consulting

Scenario: You work at a consulting firm that charges clients by the hour. Actual oversight on your time logs is minimal, and the client rarely questions itemized hours.

1. **Tactic**: Log extra half-hours here and there, spend 90 minutes but bill for two hours. Spread these increments across various tasks to avoid detection in a single massive overcharge.

2. **Justification**: "Context switching" or "follow-up emails" are intangible tasks that pad your hours.

3. **Outcome**: You appear industrious, the firm earns more revenue (assuming your boss looks the other way), and you get credit for higher billable hours. Risks include an audit or a savvy client demanding transparency.

Example 2: Manipulating Corporate Training Budgets

Scenario: Your company allocates funds for professional development, courses, certifications, or conferences. However, these budgets are often loosely tracked.

1. **Tactic**: Register for an online course. Use the budget to pay for it, but focus only on modules that interest you personally or relate to your side hustle. You get the credential or knowledge you want while the company foots the bill.

2. **Inflating Costs**: If no one's verifying the tuition breakdown, choose a slightly more expensive "premium" package that includes perks you don't necessarily use.

3. **Outcome**: You effectively gain free education without guaranteeing any direct return on investment for the company.

Example 3: Expense Report Loopholes on Business Trips

Scenario: You travel to a conference in a major city with a generous daily meal allowance (per diem).

1. **Tactic**:

   o **Max Out Per Diem**: Instead of honest receipts, you claim the full per diem. Then you dine cheaply or skip meals entirely and pocket the difference.

   o **Shared Airbnb**: Book an Airbnb with colleagues but expense a mid-range hotel cost. Split the Airbnb cost quietly among yourselves at a lower total rate.

2. **Outcome**: You return from the trip with extra cash in your pocket, money that was earmarked for travel expenses but ends up padding your wallet. The risk is minimal if your finance department doesn't demand actual receipts or if they accept broad "daily allowance" claims.

Handling Confrontations and Damage Control

As with any unethical hack, the big question is what happens if someone notices. The workplace presents unique challenges: you're dealing with colleagues you may see daily, a boss you report to, and an HR or finance department that can impose real consequences.

If Suspicions Arise

1. **Immediate Denial or Confusion**: Channel the tactics from earlier chapters. Act perplexed: "I thought that's how we always file these expenses. Did I misunderstand the policy?"

2. **Partial Admission**: If evidence is strong, consider a partial confession that frames your act as an innocent mistake. "I honestly believed it was acceptable to expense personal dinners as part of the per diem, I must have read the policy incorrectly."

3. **Diversion**: Raise a separate issue or volunteer some tangential information that shifts the conversation away from your wrongdoing. "I'm so sorry about this confusion, by the way, I uncovered an accounting discrepancy in the last quarter's travel budget that might save the company money."

Managing HR Escalations

Human Resources can be your ally or enemy, depending on how you handle them:

- **A Cooperative Stance**: If HR calls you in, express your willingness to rectify the mistake. Sometimes, repaying misused funds or promising to correct a process can ward off formal disciplinary measures.

- **Avoid Over-Explaining**: The more you talk, the more incriminating details you might reveal. Keep your statements factual and minimal, focusing on how you'll fix the perceived issue.

If you sense the situation is dire, e.g., potential termination, evaluate whether it's worth fighting to stay in a place that's discovered your unethical approach. Some employees choose to negotiate a quiet resignation or amicable separation to avoid official scandal.

The Ethical and Psychological Costs

While it can be tempting to see the workplace as a playground for cunning shortcuts, it's worth noting the unique moral and psychological pressures here:

- **Long-Term Relationships**: Your coworkers are not faceless corporations. Subverting them for personal gain can breed guilt or create a toxic environment.

- **High Stakes**: A termination on your record or a damaged professional reputation can haunt you far more than losing a store membership. The corporate realm isn't always forgiving, and word travels fast among industry peers.

- **Burnout from Deceit**: Constantly maintaining illusions of productivity and forging time-off records can be emotionally draining. Some manipulative employees eventually find themselves exhausted by the mental overhead of perpetually orchestrating these small fictions.

Ultimately, ask yourself if the incremental benefits, extra free time, slightly inflated expense reimbursements, a less demanding workload, justify the potential fallout if discovered. Much depends on your ambition, risk tolerance, and personal code of ethics (or lack thereof).

Work Smarter, Not Harder (With Caveats)

In a perfect world, promotions and raises would be earned solely through genuine hard work and merit. But workplaces, just like retail stores or financial institutions, are governed by rules and norms that can be massaged by those who dare. Whether you manipulate official policies, exploit personal connections, or simply maintain an illusion of tireless dedication, the professional environment is ripe for cunning hacks.

Yet, the stakes are undeniable: a single misstep can cost you not just money, but reputation, job security, and future prospects. Unlike small consumer scams that you can walk away from if caught, the workplace is part of your identity and livelihood. At minimum, weigh the benefits against the potential damage, both to your career and to your conscience.

Key Takeaways:

1. **Perception is Everything**: Use small cues (timed emails, visible engagement) to appear more productive than you might actually be.

2. **Policy Exploits**: Exploit lax PTO rules, expense accounts, or training budgets. The bigger the company, the more likely you can slip through the cracks.

3. **Favors and Alliances**: Build an IOU economy within the office, but tread carefully to avoid blackmail territory or cynicism from peers.

4. **Cover Your Tracks**: Keep your stories consistent, feign ignorance when challenged, and maintain plausible deniability.

5. **Assess the Risks**: Getting caught could mean job loss or reputational harm. Know your comfort zone before diving in.

Chapter 7:
Exploiting Social Events
and Public Spaces

Most people assume that invitations, tickets, or badges are absolute requirements for entry. They accept the idea that one must pay a certain fee or carry specific credentials to occupy particular spaces or receive certain perks. You, on the other hand, know better. Buildings, gatherings, and entire urban infrastructures often rely more on social conformity than ironclad verification to maintain order. Whether it's a VIP lounge at a conference, a premium seating area at a concert, or hotel amenities meant for paying guests only, there are abundant "grey zones" to exploit, provided you stay discreet, confident, and prepared with a plausible story if challenged.

In this chapter, we'll break down how to infiltrate events and conventions, how to maximize freebies, how to game the hospitality industry for upgrades and complimentary items, and how to slip under the radar in public spaces. By the end, you'll possess a full arsenal of strategies to enjoy more than you pay for, all by subtly sidestepping protocols that rely on the honor system or casual enforcement.

Events, Conferences, and Conventions

Conferences, conventions, and other large-scale events are gold mines for free items, networking opportunities, and exclusive experiences, if you know how to get in. The bigger the event, the less personal scrutiny. Most event staff just follow basic instructions: scan a badge, glance at a wristband, or check a lanyard color. They rarely suspect someone who looks like they belong.

Sneaking Past Registration and Ticket Scanners

Leverage Crowd Density

Large conventions often attract thousands of attendees. In chaotic environments, staff can't carefully scrutinize every badge or ticket. Use the following approaches:

1. **Timing Your Entrance:**

   - **Peak Rush Hours**: Arrive during the busiest times, when staff are overwhelmed by the flow of people. Act rushed yet purposeful, as if you've done this a hundred times. Handlers often wave you through rather than risk causing a bottleneck.

   - **Shift Changes:** Security or volunteer staff might rotate every few hours. If you fail on the first try, leave the queue, wait for a new set of guards or volunteers who haven't seen you yet, and attempt again.

2. **Carrying an Official-Looking Badge or Bag:**

   o **Repurposed Badges:** If you have a badge from a previous year's event, or a badge from a similar conference, clip it on a lanyard and wear it casually. In a crush of attendees, staff may not even notice the outdated date.

   o **Branded Bags or Attire:** Wearing a shirt, jacket, or tote bag with the event's logo (picked up cheaply online or from a friend who attended in previous years) can create the illusion you're officially part of the conference family.

3. **Confidence as a Key:**

   o Walk quickly, hold your phone as if you're reading urgent instructions, and avoid eye contact. If someone tries to stop you, feign frustration: "I'm running late for a panel; can we do this after?" This often flusters volunteers or junior staff enough to let you pass.

Risk and Reward

Sneaking into a paid event might save you hundreds of dollars in registration fees. However, if you're caught, the best approach is to act genuinely confused: "My badge is in my bag. I'm so sorry, I must have lost it. Let me go check." Then gracefully exit the area. Getting escorted out by security can end your day (or your entire presence at the event) for good.

Harvesting Freebies and Samples Meant for Insiders

Exhibitors love handing out freebies, keychains, tote bags, USB drives, T-shirts, even snack items, to entice potential clients. They assume that only legitimate attendees will approach their booth, so they rarely police who's taking what.

1. **Multiple Rounds:**

   o Large conventions often span multiple days. You can make a quick pass on Day 1 for initial freebies, then return on Day 2 (possibly with a different outfit or hairstyle) to grab more, especially if new staff are manning the booth.

   o If the booth has a sign-up form for freebies, use different email addresses or slightly different name variations ("Jon Smith" vs. "Jonathan Smith").

2. **Vendor Presentations and Lunch & Learns:**

   o Many conferences host "lunch and learn" sessions where vendors sponsor free meals in exchange for a short presentation. If the session doesn't require a ticket scan, simply walk in like you belong. Don't linger near the entry tables, head straight to a seat or the food line.

   o If you're questioned, claim you're an invited guest or that you received an email reminder from the vendor.

3. **Winning Raffles and Giveaways (Without a Badge):**

- o Raffles typically require you to drop a business card or fill out an entry form. If you don't have a legitimate badge, no worries. Create a stack of "business cards" with a free online generator using slightly varied personal info each time.

- o Even if the raffle rules say "must be present to win," you can stake out the time and location of the drawing. If your name is called, quickly step forward, nobody will check your badge or your ID unless the prize is extremely valuable.

Pro Tip: Many booths have tiered freebies, pens and stickers for casual passersby, nicer gifts (like branded electronics) for potential leads. Express interest in their product or service, nod and smile at their pitch, then politely mention you might need to "discuss with your team back home." They'll often hand you the premium goodie, hoping to sway your nonexistent colleagues.

VIP and Exclusive Sections

Some events host VIP lounges, behind-the-scenes tours, or exclusive after-parties. Getting in may require a special wristband or badge addition. Here's how to skirt those requirements:

1. **Identify Vulnerable Entry Points:**

   - o Often, there's more than one entrance, staff might guard the main door but leave a side entrance less monitored, especially if it's for catering or event personnel.

- o   If you notice a staff corridor, wait for a moment when workers pass through with equipment and slip in behind them.

2. **Borrow or Trade Wristbands:**

- o   If you know someone who has a VIP wristband, see if you can coordinate a swap once they're done using it. Some wristbands can be loosened and re-secured, or you can slip it off carefully over your hand and pass it along.

- o   If a friend or contact is leaving the event early, ask to take their badge. With a bit of luck and acting, no one will notice the photo or name discrepancy if you move with confidence.

3. **Fake Staff or Organizer Angle:**

- o   Wear a black T-shirt and a lanyard with a walkie-talkie (real or nonfunctional). Appear busy and purposeful, as if you're working for the event's tech crew or security. Staff rarely challenge someone who looks like they're on official duty.

Hospitality Hacks in Hotels and Restaurants

Hotels and restaurants rely on a mix of customer satisfaction and standardized rules, but they also deal with high turnover, tired staff, and varying management styles. This creates fertile ground for the cunning guest to score freebies, upgrades, and special treatment, all by exploiting oversights or well-timed complaints.

Upgrading Rooms and Meals via Complaints

Strategic Complaints

One of the classic hotel hacks involves complaining about something that might be wrong in your room or meal, often an exaggerated or entirely fabricated issue. Most hospitality managers prefer to appease you rather than argue, offering upgrades, discounts, or complimentary items to maintain a positive reputation.

1. **Minor Issues Amplified:**

   - Complain that you heard strange noises from the hallway at night or that the Wi-Fi signal was weak. Staff can't always verify these claims, so they might default to offering a partial refund or room upgrade.

   - In a restaurant, mention a slight undercooking or an unexpected flavor. Compliment the rest of the meal, but express disappointment in one aspect.

The manager may comp that dish or give you a free dessert to smooth things over.

2. **Timing is Everything:**

   o Aim for moments when staff are busy or the manager is juggling multiple tasks. They might offer a quick fix (like a free upgrade) to avoid a prolonged debate or bad online review.

   o Late-night hotel staff are often understaffed or exhausted. If you complain politely but firmly, they might expedite a room change or partial refund without too many questions.

Be Polite Yet Persistent

It's a balancing act: complain convincingly without sounding aggressive or entitled. "I'm not one to make a fuss, but I can't sleep with all this noise. Is there anything you can do to help?" This can spark empathy, especially if the staff believes you're usually easygoing.

Scoring Complimentary Items and Discounts

1. **Free Breakfast or Drinks**

   o Ask if your reservation includes complimentary breakfast (even if it normally doesn't). If the front desk staff is unsure, they might err on the side of granting it.

- o   At restaurants or bars, mention a special occasion, like a birthday or anniversary. Many places offer a free dessert or drink. If asked for ID or proof, feign surprise: "I didn't realize I needed proof it's my birthday!"

2. **Leveraging Membership and Loyalty Programs**

- o   Even if you're not a regular member, sign up for a loyalty program on the spot. Sometimes the system automatically grants a welcome perk, like a free beverage or an upgrade if available.

- o   Claim you forgot your membership number but know you have status. "I'm a Platinum member, but I don't have my card on me. Could you look me up?" If the staff can't find you, they might give you the perk anyway to keep you happy.

3. **Room Service Hacks**

- o   If you see leftover trays in the hallway with unopened drinks or sealed snacks, you could discreetly claim them. It's a small score but also a small risk.

- o   Sometimes, if you phone room service and complain about a missing or incorrect item, the staff might send a replacement or extra food to make amends, especially if they're busy and can't double-check your original order.

Hospitality Industry Insiders

If you really want to push the boundaries, you can pose as someone with industry clout:

- **Blogger or Social Media Influencer**:
  Mention you write reviews for a popular travel site or blog. Even if you have a modest following, many managers fear a negative mention. They might offer freebies or discounts to secure a favorable review.

- **Mystery Shopper Ruse**:
  Imply (subtly) you're evaluating the establishment for a parent company or for a hospitality association. This can be as simple as taking notes while you walk around, asking detailed questions, or snapping photos. Staff might treat you extra carefully, sometimes comping items to ensure a glowing report.

Risk: While less common than you might think, some savvy managers might ask for credentials or proof of your affiliation. If you can't provide it, your credibility evaporates quickly. Then you must pivot: "Oh, maybe the email was about a different location. Sorry for the confusion!"

Public Resource Manipulations

Parks, libraries, museums, public spaces designed for community benefit, often operate with minimal oversight. You can exploit this to get more than your share of free amenities, from Wi-Fi to equipment rentals, as long as you remain stealthy.

Libraries, Gyms, and Community Centers

1. **Borrowing Without a Resident ID**

    o   Some libraries let visitors check out materials or use special equipment (like 3D printers, recording studios, or meeting rooms) if they have a local ID. If you don't, say you're new in town and haven't updated your driver's license yet. They might grant a temporary pass or guest privileges.

    o   If you're in a large city with multiple branches, you can hop between them, using different addresses or ID forms, each branch might not cross-check an entire city database thoroughly.

2. **Gym "Free Trial" Loops**

    o   Many public or community gyms have low-cost daily passes or free trial periods. You could sign up multiple times with minor identity variations or alternate contact info. If there's minimal staff continuity, they may not remember you.

    o   Some facilities let you swipe a membership card for entry with no photo check. If you borrow a friend's membership card, a cursory glance by staff might be all you face.

3. **Free Classes and Workshops**

   o   Community centers offer free or low-fee classes, yoga, pottery, language exchange. If there's no strict attendance list, simply show up. If someone asks, "Are you registered?" a casual "Yes, I signed up online" might suffice, especially if the class is large and unmonitored.

Exploiting Public Wi-Fi and Power

1. **Unrestricted Wi-Fi Networks**

   o   Many public libraries, cafes, and community centers broadcast open Wi-Fi signals even after business hours. Sitting outside in your car or a nearby bench can grant you free internet indefinitely.

   o   Some cities offer municipal Wi-Fi hot zones with inconsistent login verifications. If you're prompt in refreshing the session or using a random MAC address each time, you can bypass time limits.

2. **Charging Devices in Public Outlets**

   o   Malls, airports, or train stations typically have charging stations or power outlets. While intended for travelers or waiting customers, there's usually no enforcement against simply walking in to charge your phone.

    o   If questioned, pretend you're waiting for someone who's in a store or a meeting. Appear engaged in something else, like reading or working on a laptop, to blend in.

Note: While using public Wi-Fi or outlets is generally free, watch out for locked or members-only lounges. Some airports reserve certain power stations or seating areas for specific airline members. If staff catch you, politely say you didn't realize you were in a restricted zone.

Disappearing in the Crowd

Some public spaces, busy streets, subway stations, large festivals, allow near-complete anonymity. This can be useful if you need to avoid direct scrutiny or slip in and out of events unnoticed.

- **Blend with Tour Groups**: Tour groups often wear matching stickers or lanyards. If you spot a group with minimal oversight, walk alongside them. You might gain access to group-only areas or skip lines, as staff assume you're part of the paid tour.

- **Free Rides or Park Access**: Large-scale amusements or fairs sometimes rely on wristbands or stamps. If you see someone leaving with an intact wristband, you can politely ask, "Are you done using that?" Peel it off carefully and reattach it to your wrist.

Real-World Examples and Anecdotes

1. **Concert Seat Upgrades**: At many concerts, ushers only check tickets when you first enter a section. By mid-show, they're less vigilant. You can move to a better seat row by row. If questioned, claim you got confused after visiting the restroom.

2. **Hotel Pool Hopping**: Some travelers "hotel-hop" by wearing casual pool attire and carrying a hotel-branded towel (easily acquired from the front desk earlier or found in the pool area). Staff rarely cross-check names for pool usage. You can lounge, swim, and even use the hot tub without being a registered guest.

3. **Airline Lounge Access**: Major airports often have lounges for premium cabin flyers or certain credit card holders. If you dress business-casual, carry a decoy membership card, and speak confidently, staff may give you a quick pass, especially if the lounge is crowded.

Ethical and Social Implications

Exploiting public spaces and social events might feel less predatory than ripping off a small mom-and-pop shop, particularly when dealing with large conferences, corporate hotel chains, or well-funded city projects. Still, these actions can have repercussions:

1. **Crowding Out Legitimate Users**: Taking up limited freebies or resources (like event meals or library equipment) can deprive actual paying guests or local residents who need them.

2. **Security Concerns**: Some restricted areas exist for genuine safety reasons. Blurring those lines could lead to unintended risks for you and others.

3. **Community Reputation**: If your stunts are too bold or frequent, you might be recognized or reported, tarnishing your standing if you're part of that local scene or industry.

Ultimately, the social contract depends on a basic level of honesty. People who repeatedly exploit generosity or trust can slowly erode the willingness of institutions to offer freebies and open access. Recognize that your short-term gain might contribute to stricter rules in the future.

Strategies for Discretion and Risk Management

1. **Dress the Part:**

   o For conferences, dress in business casual or the typical attire of attendees. For high-end restaurants, put on neat, upscale clothing. Looking out of place invites scrutiny.

   o If you're in a creative or tech conference, a casual T-shirt with a relevant brand or design can help you blend right in.

2. **Be Friendly but Not Suspiciously Over-eager:**

   o Greet staff with a relaxed smile, but don't linger to chat or stand out. Too much conversation can prompt them to remember your face.

   o Avoid obviously "casing" the venue, wandering around looking lost or peering at signage for rules.

3. **Exit Quickly if Challenged:**

   o Should someone confront you, "Can I see your badge?" "Are you staying at this hotel?", use a short, apologetic explanation, then leave. Don't argue or escalate.

   o Claim ignorance if cornered: "I'm sorry, I thought it was open to the public," or "My friend said we could come here." Then beat a hasty retreat.

4. **Avoid Over-Indulging:**

   o Taking advantage of a free sample table once or twice is fine. Loading up a huge bag with giveaways is more likely to get you noticed or labeled a freeloader.

   o If you slip into a hotel's continental breakfast, discreetly grab a plate or a coffee, not the entire buffet for an hour.

5. **Rotate Targets:**

o   Don't repeatedly crash the same event or the same hotel lounge. Vary your approach, location, and timing. This lowers the odds of staff recognizing you.

Looking Ahead

Exploiting social events and public spaces can yield a host of small but satisfying wins, free gear, free meals, better seats, VIP treatment. The trick is to blend in, maintain confidence, and exit gracefully if challenged. Whether you're snagging an extra dessert at a banquet or enjoying a pool meant for hotel guests only, the underlying principle remains the same: most barriers exist as polite deterrents, not absolute guardrails. If you appear to belong, act courteously, and know the system's weak spots, the gatekeepers are often too busy or disinterested to stop you.

Key Takeaways

1. **Conferences and Conventions**: Sneak in during rush periods, exploit freebies and raffles, and gain VIP access by looking official and moving with purpose.

2. **Hospitality Hacks**: Use well-timed complaints to secure upgrades, pose as an influencer, and discreetly enjoy amenities meant for paying guests.

3. **Public Resources**: Libraries, gyms, community centers, and public Wi-Fi stations can be used well beyond their intended limits, just stay polite and rotate frequently.

4. **Risk Management**: Dress the part, maintain a low profile, and retreat if you meet resistance. Overreaching or drawing attention can end your exploit swiftly.

Chapter 8:
White Lies, Half-Truths, and Guilty Silences

There comes a moment in nearly every unethical scheme, large or small, when someone asks, "Wait, is that really what happened?" In that instant, your response can either confirm their suspicions or spin the story in your favor. The ability to conceal the truth without outright lying (or at least without lying so blatantly you're easily caught) is an art form as old as human communication itself. Sometimes a well-placed omission works better than a fabricated story. Other times, you need a neat half-truth to deflect blame, or a gentle misdirection to steer attention away from delicate details.

Knowing which tactic to deploy, and how to keep your conscience quiet in the process, requires a calculated mix of psychological insight and self-control. This chapter dives into the mechanics of weaving small untruths into your daily interactions, from selective self-presentation (your "personal brand") to the finer points of staying calm under direct questioning. You'll see how to reduce suspicion, manage guilt, and maintain plausibility when you're challenged about a questionable advantage you've seized. Whether you're skipping out on fees, stepping into VIP lounges you never paid for, or padding your work-from-home hours, these mental and rhetorical defenses protect you from the bright light of scrutiny.

Personal Branding Through Omission

The Idea of a Curated Persona

In an era where everyone feels pressured to "brand" themselves, online and off, you can present a curated image that leans heavily on omission. Rather than lying about your credentials or experiences, you simply fail to mention certain details that contradict the persona you want to project. For instance, you might play up your involvement in volunteer work and quietly gloss over the fact that it ended poorly or that it was just a single afternoon event years ago. You never directly say you volunteered for months on end; you simply let people assume a longer commitment if they wish.

1. **Strategic Social Media Profiles:**

    o   Share posts that depict you as hardworking, charitable, or well-connected. Do not reveal potential red flags, like that you only worked at a charity for a few hours. People fill in the gaps with their own assumptions.

    o   Selectively delete or untag yourself from photos that undermine your cultivated image. No need to lie about your wild party days if there's no trace of them in your public-facing world.

2. **Selective Topic Shifts:**

- o When talking about your background at a
     networking event, focus on the achievements you
     want to highlight. Keep the conversation anchored
     in territory where you shine. If someone asks for
     more detail on a patchy area, pivot: "That's a long
     story, I'll share it later if we have time, but I'm
     really excited to talk about the new project I'm
     working on right now."

- o In job interviews or professional settings,
     emphasize the roles and responsibilities that make
     you appear qualified or experienced. Let them
     assume your tenure was longer or more impactful
     than it actually was, as long as you aren't explicitly
     fabricating timelines.

Why Omission Works So Well

Omission is powerful because it doesn't rely on a bald-faced lie. It thrives on others' assumptions, human beings love to fill in the blanks with the rosiest possible picture. People are often too polite or too pressed for time to dig deeper into every detail. As a result, they mentally "complete" your story in the way that best fits their own narrative or expectations. You maintain plausible deniability if something contradictory emerges: "Oh, I'm sorry; I never actually said I volunteered for six months. I only said I was part of the organization."

Deflecting Suspicion and Re-Directing Blame

The Fine Art of Shifting Focus

Deflection is about steering the conversation away from the parts that would incriminate or embarrass you. It isn't the same as denying something happened. Instead, you rely on distractions, tangents, or third-party scapegoats to shift the listener's attention. For instance, if a coworker confronts you about an odd expense on the corporate card, you might respond, "That's weird, finance has been messing up reimbursements all month. Let's see if their system glitched again." You haven't lied about your own role, but you've pointed them toward a different potential culprit.

1. **Point to a Broader Issue:**

    o If you're confronted about questionable behavior, like returning used merchandise to a store, play up a systemic flaw. "Yeah, I noticed other customers complaining, too. The store's policy is so vague; no wonder there's confusion."

    o This suggests your individual act is a symptom of a larger problem, not a discrete attempt to abuse the system.

2. **Overwhelm With Facts (on Another Topic):**

    o Some people are easily lost in a flurry of data. If they question you about whether you truly have the credentials you claim, bury them in talk of your current projects, your future plans, or statistics that are tangentially related.

o   The goal isn't to clarify the original question; it's to push it into the background until they give up pursuing it.

Redirecting Blame Upwards or Outwards

If direct blame seems imminent, someone is suspicious that you walked out of a hotel with an armload of complimentary items, they might be on the verge of confronting you or lodging a complaint. One strategy is to look above or outside your immediate circle:

- **Higher Authority:** "The front desk assured me it was fine to take these."

- **Policy Ambiguity:** "I've seen other guests do the same, so I assumed it was allowed."

- **Technical Error:** "It must be a glitch. I'd love to rectify it, but I was told the system was correct."

While these statements might contain partial truths or no truth at all, they're vaguely specific enough that the offended party might shift their anger to the "front desk," "policy," or "system" instead of pressing you.

Justifying Actions to Yourself and Others

Mastering Self-Talk to Stifle Guilt

Even the most unscrupulous among us can feel pangs of guilt from time to time. For your own psychological comfort, you may need internal scripts that rationalize what you're doing. Consider these rationalizations as mental narratives that keep cognitive dissonance at bay:

1. **Everyone Else Does It:**

   o   This classic justification helps you see your actions as part of a collective normal, not an outlier. Whether or not "everyone else" truly does it is beside the point. If you can point to a handful of acquaintances or a broad social phenomenon, you can quell your internal moral conflict.

   o   E.g., "Loads of people share streaming accounts without paying extra. I'm just doing what everyone else is doing."

2. **They Deserve It (or They Can Afford It):**

   o   Another popular angle is framing your victim (often a large corporation) as deserving to be scammed. You might tell yourself, "Company X charges exorbitant prices anyway; they won't miss a few bucks."

   o   This stance portrays your exploit as a form of economic justice or balancing the scales.

3. **Ends Justify the Means:**

   o   If your unethical hack frees up extra money you plan to use for a beneficial purpose, like caring for family or investing in a dream project, you can silence guilt by focusing on the positive outcome.

    o   "I might be bending the rules, but I'm doing it for a good reason. That has to count for something."

Presenting Rationalizations Publicly

When someone inquires about your questionable actions, you might deploy the same internal script outwardly, though carefully. Vocalizing "they can afford it" or "everyone else does it" might sound too blunt, so you repackage it:

- "I've seen a lot of people handle it this way, and the company hasn't objected."

- "I'm just trying to make ends meet. Big corporations don't exactly make it easy on the little guy."

Phrased sympathetically, you come off as a relatable figure simply navigating an unfair system. This can soften any judgment from casual onlookers or friends who might otherwise challenge you.

White Lies in Practice: Everyday Scenarios

Excuses and Alibis

Small white lies are often used to slip out of obligations or appear more upright than you actually are. Maybe you call in sick to work when you're actually spending the day at a theme park. Or you tell a friend you can't attend their party because of "family obligations," when in reality you just prefer to stay home. While these might seem trivial, they weave into a larger pattern of routine deceptions that can become second nature.

1. **Minimal Detail Policy:**

- o The less detail you provide in your fib, the safer it is. Over-elaboration draws suspicion.

- o "I'm feeling under the weather. I need a sick day." That's it. No invented symptoms or elaborate hospital stories, which might unravel if anyone follows up.

2. **Leaning on Social Politeness:**

- o Many people are too polite to pry. If you say, "I have a personal emergency," they'll typically back off. By relying on the norms of privacy and empathy, you avoid deeper scrutiny.

Product Returns and Service Complaints

Whether it's returning a used item to a store under the pretense "it was never worn" or claiming dissatisfaction with a meal you devoured, white lies grease the wheels. For a restaurant complaint, you might say, "The dish was too salty to finish," then hope the staff doesn't notice your plate is nearly empty. By keeping your tone calm and matter-of-fact, you signal you're not out to scam them; you're just reporting a defect.

- **Body Language Alignment:**

- o Appear mildly disappointed rather than outraged. A calm demeanor can convince staff you're an honest patron just looking for a fair remedy.

- o   If you seem overly theatrical, managers may suspect you're exaggerating or making something up.

Job-Related Fibbing

From inflating your prior responsibilities on a résumé to fudging the reasons you're leaving a role ("I'm seeking more growth opportunities," rather than "I was about to be fired"), these half-truths can open doors otherwise closed. Employers themselves sometimes expect a certain amount of polished spin.

- **Résumé Omissions:**

  - o   If you have short stints or embarrassing roles, leave them off entirely. Most recruiters won't question small date gaps. Should they ask, you can say you were freelancing, traveling, or caring for a family member.

- **References and Endorsements:**

  - o   If asked for references, select those who will vouch for you wholeheartedly. They don't need to know the less savory details of your work history. If you parted ways on bad terms with a manager, simply omit them.

Making the Scam Look Accidental

Feigning Ignorance or Misinterpretation

One tactic is to behave as though you were entirely unaware you were doing anything wrong. If confronted about an exploit, maybe you used multiple coupon codes that shouldn't stack, just say, "Oh, the site accepted them, so I assumed it was allowed." You haven't lied about your intentions; you've feigned ignorance of the rules. This can be more palatable than insisting it was your right to use them.

1. **Curating a Confused Persona:**

   o "I had no idea I was supposed to check out differently."

   o "Wait, I'm sorry, this was my first time using these coupons. I thought they'd just reject what wasn't allowed."

2. **Offering Quick Apologies:**

   o "I'm so sorry if I misunderstood. Let me fix that." Sincerity lowers the other person's guard and prompts them to see you as misguided rather than manipulative.

"I Must Have Made a Mistake"

Sometimes, an effective strategy is to own up to something being "wrong," yet phrase it as an honest slip. If you accidentally slip into a conference's VIP lounge and get spotted, a line like "Oh, I genuinely thought this was the main reception area" may rescue you from immediate ejection. People are kinder to mistakes than to deliberate rule-breaking.

Seeding Alternative Explanations

Preparing a Back-Up Story

If you expect your hack might draw questions, have a back-up explanation. If you've been redeeming multiple free trials of a streaming service under different email addresses, be ready in case the customer support agent flags your account. You could claim, "My roommates and I each have an account. Maybe the system is merging them somehow." Offer plausible details, names or a casual mention of your living arrangement, to sell it. Then express confusion rather than arrogance.

The Pre-Emptive Diversion

Sometimes, seeding a false or misleading story before suspicion arises deflates potential interrogation. For example, if you plan to stage multiple online returns for lightly used items, start dropping hints to friends and family about how you're "trying out a bunch of brands for an upcoming project or review." This creates a background narrative that explains the volume of returns if they happen to notice or question it.

- **Ally as a Witness:**

    o If you tell a close friend you're writing a "product comparison blog," they might vouch for you if someone else asks why you're returning so many items. They become an unknowing accomplice in propping up your cover story.

- This approach works best in personal circles or smaller communities, not for corporate or official oversight.

Navigating Internal Tensions and Practical Ethics

The Psychological Toll of Habitual Lying

Even small, repeated deceptions can pile up mentally. Each white lie demands you track what you told whom, to avoid contradicting yourself in the future. Over time, you might experience subtle stress, a low-level anxiety of being caught or having to spin new stories to cover old ones. This psychological overhead can chip away at your well-being or make you more prone to slip-ups.

- **Compartmentalize Wisely:**

  - Keep a mental or physical note of the lies you've told, especially if they impact different circles, work, friends, family. It's easy to forget you told your boss you had a sick family member when you told your colleagues you were on vacation.

  - Rehearse key lines if you sense a confrontation is likely. Feeling prepared reduces panic.

Reputation and Relationship Damage

When someone discovers you've consistently withheld the truth or twisted facts, it can devastate their trust. The fallout might be heavier in personal relationships, but it can also burn professional bridges or social networks. The short-term gains from a well-placed lie may not outweigh the long-term cost if you rely on that person's goodwill.

- **Strategic Truth-Telling Where It Counts:**

  o If you care about maintaining genuine relationships with certain friends or mentors, keep them out of your manipulative webs. Select targets or contexts where you can afford the risk of burned bridges if exposed.

  o In some workplaces or social groups, honesty and authenticity are prized. Weigh carefully whether your deceptions can remain undetected in such close-knit environments.

Noteworthy Observations

In this domain of unethical life hacks, deception often underpins the entire strategy. Yet, not every lie is equally potent or equally harmful. Sometimes, a mild omission or a half-truth can nudge you over a small hurdle without requiring full-scale fraud. The brilliance (or darkness, depending on perspective) of white lies and half-truths is how smoothly they glide under most people's moral radar. You're not forging a signature, hacking a database, or openly swindling anyone. You're simply letting others assume the story they want to hear and adjusting a few details to your advantage.

No matter how comfortable you get with these tactics, it's wise to maintain a sense of self-awareness. Sliding too deep into routine dishonesty can erode your personal relationships, your mental peace, and even your sense of identity. Part of the skill is knowing when to put on the brakes, especially with people or institutions you might genuinely care about. Still, if you're already treading the path of cunning exploitation, these tactics provide a safer cushion between your exploits and exposure. A well-timed half-truth or a neatly deployed "guilty silence" can keep you in the clear long enough to reap the benefits you seek, with minimal pushback or penalty.

Embrace the subtle artistry of deception if you must, just be prepared to manage the illusions you weave, and remember to keep track of which story you're telling to whom. After all, the sharpest lies are the ones that look most like the truth, leaving just enough space for people to fill in the blanks themselves.

Chapter 9:
Ensuring Long-Term Gains Without Burnout

Up to this point, you've accumulated a range of sneaky strategies for extracting small (and sometimes not-so-small) wins from life, bending rules at work, orchestrating subtle manipulations in social and public spaces, collecting freebies, and covering your tracks with half-truths. But to sustain any series of unethical exploits over the long haul, you'll need a careful game plan. After all, even a cunning "rogue" can't continuously run in circles, pushing boundaries, without risking burnout or eventual detection. This chapter digs into the practical considerations of pacing and endurance: how to scale up your activities gradually without drawing extra attention, how to rotate targets and tactics so your patterns aren't obvious, and how to weigh the risk-reward ratio so you don't overextend yourself.

There's a balancing act here. If you move too slowly or too timidly, you might miss opportunities and fail to enjoy the full benefits of your cunning. But if you dive in headfirst, hammering the same store's return policy or running the same subscription free-trial hack over and over, eventually you will stand out, or a system will tighten in response. Your best bet is to cultivate a long-term perspective, leveraging your knowledge and skill in ways that keep you perpetually on the right side of plausible deniability. From rotating your targets to knowing when to exit a scam, this chapter offers a blueprint for consistent gains while minimizing the psychological, social, and legal toll of your exploits.

Scaling Up Your Tactics Gradually

Avoiding the Temptation of the "All-In" Approach

When you first discover a new exploit, a glitch on a shopping site that allows multiple promo code stacks, or a workplace expense loophole that goes unchecked, you might be tempted to go big immediately, raking in the maximum benefit before the loophole is patched. This impulsive approach can lead to dramatic wins, but it also raises your profile. If you trigger an automated fraud alert or an overeager manager's curiosity, the gravy train can abruptly derail.

1. **Start With Small Wins**

    o   Before launching a major spree (like ordering five different laptops to return them or traveling business class on your company's dime), do a small-scale test. Confirm the exploit works reliably. Maybe buy a single discounted item through the glitch, or slip just one personal dinner expense under the corporate card radar. If it goes unnoticed, you've validated the approach.

o   This strategy also helps you gauge your comfort
    level. A small initial score is less likely to cause you
    panic and second-guessing. Jumping into a large-
    scale con from day one can be emotionally
    overwhelming, fueling potential slip-ups due to
    stress or inexperience.

2. **Incremental Intensification**

    o   Once you confirm the method works, slowly ramp
        up. For instance, if you're exploiting multiple
        email addresses for streaming-service free trials,
        don't create twenty addresses overnight. Instead,
        add a new address each month, steady, subtle, and
        less likely to be flagged as suspicious.

    o   In a workplace setting, if you're quietly padding
        your hours or inflating expense reports, increase
        them gradually. Billing an extra 15 minutes here
        and there is less suspicious than suddenly jumping
        from 40 hours a week to 60 without explanation.

3. **Adaptive Experimentation**

    o   The advantage of gradual escalation is that you can
        watch for warning signs. If a website changes its
        checkout flow, or your employer's finance
        department starts auditing more receipts, you'll
        detect the shift before you commit to a large-scale
        abuse.

    o   Keep an eye on official communications, such as new policy announcements or system updates, that might indicate the company or vendor has caught on to certain patterns. Pull back or switch tactics if you see a new emphasis on "preventing fraudulent returns" or "clamping down on expense misuse."

Why Pacing Matters

People are more alert to drastic changes than to slow, subtle shifts. If your household suddenly starts receiving a massive stack of packages for "product testing," nosy neighbors or roommates might talk. If your boss notices you're suddenly expensing lavish meals every night, they'll raise an eyebrow. By pacing yourself, you blend into the background: a consistent, low-level trickle of small gains that compound over time without triggering a big reaction.

Rotating Targets and Methods

How Repetition Breeds Scrutiny

One of the quickest ways to get caught is to overuse a single exploit or repeatedly target the same company, vendor, or person. Patterns stand out. If a store's return desk recognizes you every time you stroll in with high-ticket items, they'll start to remember your face. A subscription platform might detect multiple accounts tied to the same IP address or payment method. Your manager could notice that all your expense claims center on one suspicious type of "client meal." If you're constantly using the same tactic in the same place, you increase your risk exponentially.

1. **Establish a Rotation Schedule**

   o Keep a mental or written log of where and when you've exploited a certain policy or perk. If you returned items to Store A this month, try a different chain next time. You can come back to Store A in a few months once staff turnover or memory fades.

   o With online tactics, like stacking discounts or signing up for free trials, rotate your email addresses, payment cards, and even your IP addresses (via VPN). That way, each "account" looks unique. If you always sign up from the same device or address, it's easier for the system to spot a pattern.

2. **Diversify the Tactics**

   o If you rely solely on complaining about hotel rooms for an upgrade, eventually you'll face a manager who either recognizes you or is simply less accommodating. Next time, consider a different angle: present a loyalty status, claim a corporate rate, or ask about an under-advertised package deal.

   o Apply this principle across all your hustles. If you're consistently draining freebies from a particular coffee shop, switch to the local bakery for a while. Minimizing repeated behavior not only reduces suspicion but also keeps your approach flexible.

3. **Network-Level Variation**

   o For large corporate entities with multiple brands (like a chain of stores under a single parent company), your data might be shared across these stores. If you exploit Company X in City A, doing the same trick at Company X in City B could link your accounts. In these cases, try the same hack on a different parent corporation, or bounce between smaller chains that don't share data.

Finding the Sweet Spot of Variety

You don't want to juggle so many angles that you lose track or make sloppy errors. The key is to have just enough diversity in your targets and methods to avoid detection, but not so many that you overwhelm yourself. For instance, a rotating cycle of three or four streaming services might be plenty to maintain perpetual free trials. A quick mental or digital note can remind you which one you canceled last, so you don't inadvertently re-sign up too soon under a suspicious pattern.

Balancing the Risk-Reward Ratio

Understanding "Hack Fatigue"

Constantly playing the angles can be mentally draining. You must stay vigilant, keep stories straight, and track rotating methods, especially if you're mixing personal, workplace, and public-space exploits. This can lead to what some call "hack fatigue": the sense that you're burning too much mental energy for diminishing returns. The more complex your web of manipulations, the greater the chance of an unforced error.

1. **Assess Time Spent vs. Gains**

    o   If you find yourself devoting hours to orchestrating and covering up a particular hustle that nets you $10 in savings, ask: "Is this really worth the time and stress?" Some people enjoy the game, seeing it as a challenge. Others grow resentful of the overhead. Keep a running mental tally of which exploits actually pay off in proportion to the effort.

    o   For instance, gaming airline loyalty programs to snag a free upgrade once a year might be worth it if it only requires minimal extra steps. But if you're meticulously manufacturing flight segments and booking hidden-city tickets every few weeks to inch your loyalty status higher, the mental burden can become enormous.

2. **Setting Personal Limits**

    o   It's easy to escalate from minor coupon stacking to full-blown identity juggling. Before you inch too far, define what you are and aren't willing to risk, legally, financially, or ethically. If forging documents crosses your personal boundary, make that a hard stop. If you're comfortable returning items but not with defrauding insurance, keep it that way.

o This personal line also helps you gauge which tactics are safe for you psychologically. Some people can rationalize minor consumer "cheats" but suffer guilt when manipulating colleagues at work. Knowing your threshold helps you avoid internal turmoil.

3. **Watch for Tells of Escalating Risk**

o Are you receiving more shipping confirmation emails for your various alias accounts than you can manage? Did a store manager ask you pointed questions about your frequent returns? Did your boss send a memo about "tightening expense protocols"? Each of these signals rising suspicion or stricter rules. If you keep pushing at that point, you might tip from "smart cheat" to "likely to be caught."

o When you see the risk intensify, either pause or shift to a different tactic or target. A well-timed exit from a particular hustle can save you from a crackdown.

The "Quit While You're Ahead" Principle

Many gamblers lose everything by failing to leave the table when they're up. The same can happen in unethical life hacks. A glitch in a website might let you stack discount codes for 50% off, and you exploit it ten times with no issue. If you get greedy and try for the eleventh time, you might be the one who triggers an automated review. Knowing when to walk away, especially when you've already reaped a decent gain, is a hallmark of longevity in the rogue's game. The difference between small-time cunning and a major bust often hinges on one exploit too many.

Avoiding Burnout and Maintaining Stealth

Emotional and Psychological Self-Care

Successfully navigating a world of rule-bending requires more than cunning; it also demands mental resilience. Constantly lying or obfuscating can strain relationships and cause internal stress. You might find yourself anxious around the possibility of being exposed or tired of always "spinning" your actions.

1. **Separating Normal Life from "Rogue Life"**

   o   As much as possible, compartmentalize your tactics so they don't dominate your entire mindset. If you're scanning for angles 24/7, you might never truly relax.

   o   Create deliberate downtime: once you finish orchestrating a hack, like snagging free conference tickets, allow yourself to enjoy the result without obsessing over the next exploit. In other words, treat your cunning as a tool, not an addiction.

2. **Maintaining Trust with Key People**

   o   If you have close friends or family who disapprove of your methods, decide whether it's worth lying to them or if you'll maintain transparency (to an extent). Having at least one confidant can relieve some emotional burden, but be aware of the risk that they might judge you or accidentally expose you.

   o   In the workplace, try not to drag unsuspecting coworkers into your web. Manipulating them might yield short-term gains but can severely damage your sense of belonging if they discover your ruse. Aim to keep personal relationships outside the crossfire of your hustle if you value those connections.

3. **Recognizing Signs You Need a Break**

   o   If you're losing sleep worrying about an audit or a store manager's suspicions, you may be pushing too far.

   o   If you find yourself forgetting which name you used or which version of a story you told, you might be overextending your mental capacity.

Mistakes become more likely when you're juggling too much.

- o This is your cue to pause or scale back. Focus on a low-profile tactic for a while, or just take a break from hustling altogether until you feel calm and grounded again.

Mastering the Art of "Just Enough"

Burnout often creeps in when people fixate on maximizing every possible advantage. If you try to exploit every freebie, every discount, every policy gap you see, you'll drown in complexity. By contrast, focusing on the few most rewarding, lowest-risk methods can keep you satisfied without turning your entire life into a never-ending con.

- **Quality Over Quantity**: Pick the hacks that yield tangible, worthwhile benefits. If you're going to risk being sneaky at a store, do it where the payoff is something you truly value, like a significant discount on groceries or electronics, rather than a couple of dollars off.

- **Building a Steady Flow**: Instead of chasing one huge score, cultivate a handful of moderate exploits that quietly add up. Maybe free streaming rotations, a return policy hustle once a month, the occasional complaint at a hotel for an upgrade, enough to feel like you're winning, but not so much that you're on anyone's radar as a serial abuser.

Knowing When to Stop Pushing Your Luck

Sunk Costs vs. Fresh Starts

As you refine your ability to cheat various systems, you may grow attached to certain tactics, especially if they've worked well in the past. But all good things come to an end, and a big part of sustaining your overall success is recognizing when a particular hustle has run its course. If a store implements stricter ID checks at returns, or if your workplace adopts new software that monitors expense claims in detail, clinging to the old method can lead you right into trouble.

- **Accept Evolving Rules**: Corporations and employers are not static. They learn from abuses, update policies, and install better oversight. Don't take it personally; it's just the natural cat-and-mouse cycle. A trick that was gold last year might be a liability now.

- **Pivot Instead of Persevere**: If the environment changes, don't waste time forcing an exploit that no longer works smoothly. That's usually how you get caught. Instead, explore fresh angles or refine older tactics that remain under the radar.

Managing Ego and Overconfidence

Once you've racked up a string of successful hacks, maybe you've been living on discounted or free subscription services for years, or you've traveled extensively on the company's dime, it's easy to fall prey to overconfidence. You might start believing you're untouchable or that you're "smarter" than everyone else. This mindset can be dangerous.

1. **Watch Out for Sloppy Mistakes**

    o   Complacency leads to leaving paper trails, forgetting to hide your IP, or telling the same half-truth to two different people who might compare notes.

    o   Keep in mind that your success so far might be due to others not caring enough to dig deeper. That can change abruptly if the stakes get high or if you push too far.

2. **Stay Humble in Your Exploits**

    o   Restrain yourself from bragging to peers about how you "beat" the system. Even trusted friends could let something slip accidentally.

    o   Remember that many gatekeepers, store managers, corporate accountants, membership coordinators, are professionals who deal with cunning attempts daily. They might not always show it, but they can piece together patterns if you get too bold.

3. **Accept a Quiet Win**

    o   When something goes well, resist the urge to up the ante. Keep your successes modest, and don't give your targets a reason to investigate.

- o   A sense of perspective is crucial: an occasional unplanned upgrade, waived fee, or free item can be a small but steady stream of wins. Reaching for something huge, like orchestrating a multi-thousand-dollar insurance claim, carries a far bigger risk profile that could upend your entire run.

Inching Toward a Strategic Exit

The Temporary Retreat

Sometimes, the best way to stay undetected is to deliberately lie low for a while. If you sense heightened scrutiny, like your boss's boss asking for itemized receipts, or a store cashier making notes on your return record, it might be time for a temporary retreat. Disappear from that scheme, or from that store, for a month or two. Shift your focus to other avenues until the heat cools down.

1.   **Plan for a Future Comeback**

   - o   After a break, conditions might revert to normal. Staff turnover is common in many retail and hospitality sectors; new employees won't recognize you.

   - o   If a policy was temporarily tightened, companies often loosen it again once the wave of misuse passes. Keep an eye on public forums or online chatter to see if people report changes.

2. **Creating a "Pivot Point"**

   o Use your lull to research new or emerging exploits. The online world is always providing new subscription services, referral bonuses, and loyalty programs. Even your workplace might roll out fresh policies or benefits. If you're alert, you can pivot to a novel scheme that hasn't been tested yet.

   o Sometimes, a short break re-energizes you, letting you approach hustling with renewed creativity rather than fatigue or sloppiness.

Gradual Reduction of Cheating

A few people decide eventually to reduce or even cease their unethical tactics. Maybe you've achieved a certain level of financial stability, or the game no longer excites you. Perhaps you've formed relationships you don't want to jeopardize. Easing off your exploits can be a graceful way to protect what you've gained.

- **Phasing Out Risky Methods**: If your job changes or you switch companies, that might be a good time to discard old workplace manipulations. Start fresh without a backlog of questionable expense claims.

- **Enjoying the Wins Without Doubling Down**: You can maintain a handful of low-risk freebies, like rotating email addresses for streaming services, if it's become second nature. But drop the more elaborate cons that require daily vigilance. This partial step-back can preserve your sense of cleverness without the burdensome overhead.

Some Things to Consider

Long-term success in unethical hacks isn't just about discovering a single golden tactic. It's about learning to pace yourself, scale up carefully, and remain flexible. The world changes: businesses adapt, technology evolves, and you may find your personal life or moral compass shifting as well. By rotating targets, managing your risk profile, and knowing when to walk away, you can sustain a relatively steady flow of gains without imploding under scrutiny or stress.

If you started this journey fascinated by small hustles, you might now see the broader strategic mindset required to maintain them indefinitely. Patience and discipline matter just as much as cunning. Small, incremental steps tend to draw fewer eyes than dramatic leaps, and occasional breaks can reset any suspicion that has begun to accumulate around you.

This chapter brings you closer to the point where knowledge, practice, and prudence intersect. Having gathered so many hacks, manipulations, and scripts for deception, you're well-equipped to operate under the radar for as long as you choose, provided you can handle the psychological demands and remain savvy about shifting landscapes. The next (and final) piece of the puzzle will touch on larger reflections: the moral and personal consequences of a life spent navigating the gray zones, and how these rogue skills might be repurposed or abandoned if you ever decide it's time to clean up your act.

Chapter 10:
Reflecting on Morality, Consequences, and Control

After exploring the world of hidden opportunities, loopholes, and social manipulations, you may find yourself wrestling with bigger questions: **Why do these tactics feel so tempting? How far is too far? What happens if I push my luck and everything unravels?** This chapter takes a step back from the practical how-tos and looks at the bigger picture, the moral and emotional complexities behind unethical life hacks, the potential fallout if things go sideways, and how (and why) you might choose to walk away. Far from a simple condemnation or endorsement, the goal here is to spur self-awareness. True power comes not just from knowing how to break the rules but also from understanding the broader landscape of consequence and responsibility in which those rules exist.

Reevaluating the Gains and the Hidden Costs

There's an unspoken assumption running through each of the strategies in this book: "If you can get away with it, why not?" At first glance, minor deceptions, like reusing a free trial or returning used items, appear almost victimless. You're not physically harming anyone, and large companies might not feel the financial pinch. But pause to consider the systemic effect and the personal toll:

1. **Minor Offenses, Major Patterns**

   o A small exploit may cost a company just a few dollars, but if thousands of people use the same trick, it can escalate into a notable financial loss. Businesses then tighten policies, raise prices, or become more adversarial to honest customers.

   o In a workplace setting, once you learn to cheat performance metrics or inflate expenses, you can't unsee those shortcuts. Each small success encourages you to go a step further, blurring the line between subtle advantage and overt fraud.

2. **Erosion of Trust**

   o Even if you're seldom caught, persistent rule-bending can change how you view other people (and yourself). Relationships suffer when you suspect others might be doing the same to you. You might start assuming everyone is pulling some angle.

   o Among colleagues or friends, if someone discovers your manipulations, they may no longer trust you, even if they don't outright confront you. Emotional distance and quiet suspicion can grow.

3. **Emotional and Cognitive Weight**

- o Constant vigilance is draining. Tracking lies, cover stories, and multiple identities demands cognitive resources. Instead of relaxing, you remain on guard, monitoring the narrative you've spun.

- o Guilt might creep in, even if you rationalize your actions. Certain methods of self-talk, like "everyone else does it," or "the company can afford it", can crumble under stress. Nagging doubt can undercut your sense of peace or self-worth.

Morality's Shifting Lines

For some people, moral boundaries are rigid: "Stealing is stealing, period." Others see them as highly situational: "Bending a return policy isn't the same as robbing a local business at gunpoint." In reality, the moral continuum is complicated. Where you personally draw the line might depend on context, perceived harm, or scale of benefit. A few factors often shape these internal negotiations:

1. **Upbringing and Personal Values**

   - o Family teachings, cultural norms, and life experiences can make you more or less tolerant of rule-bending. If you grew up in a tough environment with minimal resources, you might view small-scale scams as survival tactics.

   - o Conversely, someone raised in a strict moral or religious household might recoil at the idea of any dishonesty, even minor.

2. **Perceived Victims**

   - Many people justify certain hacks, like complaining for a free hotel upgrade, on the grounds that a big corporation or chain "doesn't suffer." But the moral calculus changes if you're exploiting small local shops or unsuspecting individuals. Taking advantage of a mom-and-pop store's lenient return policy can feel very different from gaming the system at a national retail giant.

   - Personalizing the "victim" tends to influence whether you feel guilty. If you encounter a friendly store clerk or a kind customer service representative, you may hesitate to push them too far.

3. **Magnitude of Consequence**

   - Grabbing a second free sample doesn't carry the same weight as orchestrating a multi-thousand-dollar insurance fraud. The question becomes: At what point do you feel you've crossed a threshold into real wrongdoing? Each person's threshold is different, and it can shift over time.

4. **Social and Cultural Influence**

   - Norms vary. In some environments, questionable practices are commonplace, like nepotism, tip-bribing for upgrades, or "unofficial" side deals. If everyone else does it, you might see less moral friction in following suit. But if you move to a setting where honesty is highly valued, you might feel more reluctant or face stronger social penalties if caught.

When the Bill Comes Due

Even the savviest manipulator can face consequences. An unexpected audit, a slip of the tongue, a suspicious coworker, or a store's new security measure can unravel months or years of low-level grifts. The fallout might range from mild embarrassment to career-ending scandal, depending on the scope of your exploits.

1. **Social Repercussions**

   o Friends or colleagues may distance themselves if they see you as untrustworthy. In tight-knit communities, word spreads. A single exposure of your methods could cost you valuable relationships.

   o Family disappointment can be devastating. If loved ones discover you've lied about finances or manipulated the system, their perception of your character might change permanently.

2. **Professional Downside**

   o Being caught cheating at work often leads to immediate termination. In some industries, a reputation for dishonesty can blacklist you, making it tough to find new opportunities.

o   If you face legal action, like being sued for fraud or embezzlement, future employers will see that on your record, complicating your career trajectory.

3. **Legal and Financial Dangers**

   o   Not all hacks are illegal, but some skirt the edges. Using false identities, forging documents, or defrauding a business can invite legal scrutiny.

   o   Penalties can escalate quickly. What starts as a minor exploit (like returning items under false pretenses) could, in certain jurisdictions, become a criminal matter if the cumulative loss is high enough.

4. **Collateral Damage**

   o   Even if you avoid direct punishment, increased security measures or stricter policies can inconvenience everyone. For instance, if you and others over-abuse a generous store return policy, the store may tighten rules, hurting ordinary customers.

   o   Within a company, your team could face blame if your expense manipulations are discovered, breeding resentment if others get caught in the crossfire.

The Fear of Exposure

Many cunning individuals live in a persistent (often subconscious) state of fear. Even small-scale hustles can trigger disproportionate anxiety because you're aware that your entire reputation or livelihood might hinge on staying undetected. This fear can manifest in subtle ways:

1. **Hypervigilance**

   - You might check your email repeatedly for signs of policy updates or watch your manager's body language for hints they suspect something. This constant vigilance can breed paranoia.

   - Some develop an unhealthy suspicion of others, projecting their own deceitful habits onto friends or coworkers.

2. **Stress and Second-Guessing**

   - Each time you benefit from a questionable move, you wonder, "Will this be the time I'm caught?" If you thrive on that adrenaline, it might feel exciting at first, but over months or years, the stress accumulates.

3. **Reluctance to Seek Genuine Help**

   - If a big problem arises, financial, medical, or legal, people who know you as a trickster might hesitate to step in. They might suspect your "crisis" is another fabricated ruse. Over time, you can become isolated.

Balancing Personal Agency and Ethical Lines

If you choose to continue employing unethical tactics, you might at least want to develop a framework for deciding how, when, and where to apply them. This can preserve some sense of control and mitigate harm:

1. **Defining a Personal Code**

    o   Even within a world of rule-bending, you can set personal guardrails: no scams that target small businesses, no deception that harms vulnerable individuals, no pushing colleagues into uncomfortable positions.

    o   This code can help you sleep easier, knowing you operate within self-imposed boundaries.

2. **Self-Awareness and Self-Correction**

    o   Check in with yourself periodically. If the moral or emotional toll grows too heavy, consider scaling back. Just because a hack is available doesn't mean you have to use it relentlessly.

    o   Some people adopt a "once a month" or "only if I really need it" policy. By treating unethical hacks as last-resort solutions rather than daily habits, you reduce emotional burnout.

3. **Maintaining Authentic Relationships**

   o If you compartmentalize your manipulations away from your personal and family life, you can preserve genuine trust where it matters most. Keep your circles separate: the people who know you intimately might never see your rogue side, and vice versa.

   o This approach, however, has its own risks. Leading a "double life" can become another source of tension if lines blur.

Repurposing These Skills for 'Good'

Interestingly, many abilities honed through unethical hacking, sharp observation, creative thinking, persuasive communication, can be redirected in socially acceptable or even benevolent ways:

1. **Legitimate Negotiation and Sales**

   o If you're adept at reading body language and framing requests, you can excel in sales, client management, or negotiation roles without outright deception. Persuasion is not inherently unethical; it becomes problematic only when twisted toward fraudulent ends.

2. **Problem-Solving and Efficiency**

   o Identifying system weaknesses can translate into a career in process optimization or cybersecurity. "White hat" hackers use similar tactics to find vulnerabilities and strengthen organizational defenses.

o   Within a legitimate role, your knack for spotting shortcuts might let you streamline real processes rather than exploit them, benefiting everyone.

3. **Advocacy and Reform**

o   Understanding how rules can be bent or broken gives you insight into writing better, fairer policies. You might become an advocate, pushing for consumer protections or fighting exploitative corporate practices. Sometimes, reformed rogues become the most passionate whistleblowers or policy reformers.

4. **Mentoring or Teaching**

o   People who've learned how to game the system, then chosen to step away, can mentor others, help them understand both the temptations and the dangers. Real-life cautionary tales can have significant impact on younger or more naive peers.

Walking Away from the Grey

Deciding to step back from unethical behavior can be as slow or abrupt as you like. Some discover a single event, a close call or a wake-up call, shifts their perspective. Others ease out gradually, letting old hustles fade without returning to them:

1. **The Sudden Break**

- o This can occur when you almost get caught, or someone you respect confronts you. You realize the risk or moral weight is no longer worth it. You discard your myriad email aliases, pay for subscriptions legitimately, and accept paying retail price sometimes.

- o The challenge is resisting relapse. If unethical hacks became part of your identity, you might feel a sense of loss or boredom without them. Filling that gap with new hobbies or pursuits can help.

2. **A Gradual Shift**

- o Maybe you cut back your exploits to the bare minimum, just a small consumer hack here or there. Over time, you might find you rely on them less frequently.

- o The more you invest in legitimate activities, the less time and motivation you have for orchestrating manipulative schemes. You might even discover surprising satisfaction in achieving goals transparently.

3. **Substituting Thrills**

- o Some people who thrive on the "rush" of bending rules turn to alternative, risk-based hobbies: adventure sports, poker, or strategic games that channel that energy into a setting where the rules exist to be played with, legally.

o   It can be liberating to realize you can challenge yourself or flirt with adrenaline without stepping into ethically fraught territory.

Bigger Possibilities for Personal Agency

All these hacks, manipulations, and strategic exploits revolve around one principle: **You're not resigned to the rules as they are presented.** This mindset can hold a surprising silver lining outside of unethical contexts: an awareness that the world is more flexible than it appears, and that creative, persistent effort can shape your reality.

1. **Entrepreneurial Vision**

   o   If you can see angles nobody else sees, you may transform that perspective into a legitimate enterprise, developing unconventional solutions or pioneering niche markets.

   o   Instead of short-term freebies, you might chase long-term success and autonomy through a real business that thrives on your innovative thinking, not on deception.

2. **Empowering Community Efforts**

   o   Civic engagement or local activism often requires out-of-the-box strategies to break through bureaucratic inertia. Your ability to identify loopholes in city regulations could become a tool for positive change (like establishing a community garden in an overlooked zone).

o   Even if you remain ethically ambiguous, you might direct some of your cunning toward community improvements that align with your sense of fairness.

Some Final Thoughts

A life of small hustles and cunning manipulations need not define your entire existence or moral character, unless you choose to let it. The real power you've gained from exploring these tactics is the awareness that most rules and boundaries in life are more permeable than they seem. Whether you continue to exploit them for personal gain or redirect your talents toward building more equitable systems is, ultimately, up to you.

Your decision may shift with time, circumstance, or personal growth. Some readers might embrace these methods as a lifelong strategy, comfortable with the trade-offs. Others might dabble, experience moral reservations, and back off. Still others might see these tactics as a stepping-stone to more profound insights about human behavior and social systems.

Regardless of your path, an essential takeaway is that ethical lines are rarely as clear-cut as society makes them out to be. You now have a front-row view of the fluid moral territory where everyday hustles happen, and with that knowledge comes responsibility: not just to shield yourself from consequences, but also to decide who you want to be in a world that offers a constant interplay between rigid structure and pliable loopholes.

Where you go from here is your choice. You could refine your mastery of these strategies, push the boundaries further, and see just how far cunning can carry you, or you might channel the same skillset into forging a different, more transparent path. The question isn't which option is "right," but which option resonates with your evolving sense of self, your tolerance for risk, and your vision of what a fulfilling life looks like.

Top 100 Unethical Life Hacks

1. If you're stuck on an annoying call, put your phone on airplane mode instead of just hanging up. The other person will see "call failed" instead of "call ended"

2. If you live someplace with a coin operated laundry, look up the washer/dryer model on eBay and order a key for it. You can open the control panel that allows you to start the cycle.

3. If the person sitting in front of you on a flight reclines their seat all the way back and leaves you with no room, turn on the air above you to full blast and point it at the top of their head.

4. Save business cards of people you don't like. If you ever hit a parked car accidentally, just write "sorry" on the back and leave it on the windshield.

5. Give your kids a bag of coal each for Christmas this year. When they cry just tell them Santa is wrong and you'll get it sorted. Once the shops open, buy what they asked for. They will think you are a legend and Santa is a dick. You will also get the presents for half price.

6. If you're initiating a divorce, secretly arrange consultations with ALL the best divorce attorneys in your area before choosing one and filing. Once they have met with you, even briefly, they are considered biased and will have to recuse themselves from representing your spouse.

7. If you ever get caught sleeping at your desk at work then say "They told me at the Blood Bank that this would happen" when asked for a reason.

8. If a computer illiterate relative or friend asks you to fix their slow computer, boost their cursor speed by a notch or two. They'll instantly notice a difference and thank you.

9. When you give someone a gift card as a gift, write down the card number and code. Then after a year or two, check the balance and if they hadn't used it yet, just use it yourself. They obviously won't know or care.

10. If you live near a US military base, it's a really good idea to install Tinder. Most military girlfriends and wives are very sexual, and their partners are typically deployed for at least a year.

11. If you glue a dead wasp to the palm of your hand, you can hit your boss on the back of the head as hard as you like and act like you saved him.

12. If you accidentally scratch someone's car, write a note in shaky handwriting saying you are 5 years old and fell off your bike. Then leave $5 saying it's all you had.

13. If you come across a dating profile begging for money, send them a request for the same amount instead of a gift. Many times they're too careless to read and will automatically accept it because they assume another desperate guy is sending cash.

14. As a parent of a baby, smell their diaper. If you DON'T smell poop, say, "Woah, somebody has a poopy diaper. "Then take them to the other room and pretend to change them. Then the next time they poop tell your spouse, "It's your turn. I changed them last time."

15. Want your commercial to be seen by millions of people for free? Put it on YouTube with the title "The commercial the Superbowl refused to run."

16. In your last year of college "lose" your student ID and get a new one. The exp date will reset and you can get another 4 years of discounts.

17. If you have a significant unexplained employment gap that is hurting your resume claim that you were providing full time end of life care for a grandparent (or other older relative).

18. Buy the cheapest tickets available for a sporting event. Once inside, check Ticketmaster and StubHub for better seats that didn't sell and go sit there.

19. Concerned about unvaccinated children spreading infection? Start rumors amongst antivaxxers that exposure to vaccinated children can cause their unvaccinated children to develop autism.... the antivaxxers will be sure to keep their children at a safe distance.

20. If you decide to adopt kids, tell them that if anyone makes fun of them for being adopted, they should say "At least I was wanted. You were probably a mistake, and your parents didn't have the heart to tell you."

21. Donate to homeless shelters in the next town over. Many homeless people tend to go where there are available services, and this will reduce the number of homeless in your town.

22. Make your edibles in the shape of dog treats and take them anywhere you want. If a drug dog finds them, his handler will just think he's being a silly boy.

23. Ever need to go to the hospital? Don't bring your ID and don't give them your real name or address.

They can't bill if they don't know who you really are. Yet they still must treat you.

24. Whenever buying something online, try using the coupon code "military". Many sites have a military discount and doesn't require any proof of military service.

25. If your company doesn't pay you for sick leaves or doesn't permit you to take sick leave; show up at work with a flu and *accidentally* infect everybody. They will eventually change policies.

26. Keep hydrated at work. You'll need to take a lot of bathroom breaks. This will make up for all the breaks smokers get. Might as well double up and start smoking.

27. Paper due at 11:59? Nowhere close to being done? Submit a paper you've done for another class and then use the time between then and when your professor emails you saying: "Oops! Looks like you submitted the wrong paper"; to work on your actual paper.

28. Learn how to read braille, create an answer sheet for a test, and put it in your hoodie pocket. You can feel the answers with your fingers without looking away from your test.

29. Need friends? Create an attractive fake tinder profile of the opposite sex, start leading on a bunch of people, arrange a date with all of them on the same time, same place. Show up as well. Announce that they must have pulled a prank on all of you and suggest you all go drinking together.

30. If you plan on going to prison, learn to cut hair. Barbers are greatly appreciated by other inmates and you'll likely be spared when it comes to prison violence.

31. Need a discount for an online purchase? Try variations of "sorry", "sorry15", "sorry20", etc. Companies will often have unadvertised coupon codes available to give to customers for faulty products or shipping mistakes.

32. Don't want to get caught plagiarizing off of Wikipedia? Translate the article to French, then Hindi, then back to English. Chip off grammatical errors and get praised for your hard work.

33. If you don't want to make a call but may later need to prove that you, in fact, did make a call but they didn't pick up, turn airplane mode on and make a call.

34. Want to get into a gated community and don't know the code? Try 9911. Most communities use it as a backup code for emergency services to get in quickly.

35. If a website requires you to enter payment information before getting a free trial, create an account on the Spanish or Belgium PayPal since those don't require you to enter a credit card to create the account, and then just add it to your payment info.

36. Starting a new job? No matter what the reality is you now have four, alive grandparents. Use this for when you absolutely need time off as most companies will give you extended paid leave for bereavement.

37. Have a racist Grandmother? Photoshop a picture of your sibling with a black man or woman and tell her they're engaged. She will take them out of the will, and you'll get a bigger share of the loot.

38. Tell your friends that you've made them a partial life insurance beneficiary. They'll feel obligated to do the same for you and will only find out you lied if you die first.

39. Want to cut into another lane of traffic but nobody will let you in? Cut in front of a Tesla, autopilot will force the car to stop.

40. If you work in retail, make a fake e-mail and write an e-mail to your boss and store praising yourself.

41. Don't get caught by your boss reading news or sports articles on your computer at work. Quickly copy the content of the article into an email and read it from there. Your boss will think you are dealing with an intensive email and will leave you alone.

42. If you're driving next to a cop with drugs in your car and are trying to act normal, pick your nose. Your body language shows you aren't concerned with anyone around you. The last thing you'd ever do if you were paranoid about a cop next to you is pick your nose.

43. Register to vote with the political party you do not align with. Screw up redistricting efforts, bias polling numbers, make outreach less efficient, vote against the front runner in a primary, and in the end you can still vote for your favorite candidate.

44. If you are a small business owner with a significant competitor, hire homeless people to bother their customers.

45. If your coworker calls out of work sick, you can do the same 1-3 days later. Your boss will think you have the same thing and it's "going around the office." In fact, most of the time, your boss will do the same thing shortly after you. It's the fake flu.

46. If you see someone shoplifting from superstores this holiday season, just mind your own damn business. Those places don't pay you to prevent their product loss.

47. Had a good first date from a dating app? Report the person in the app so their account gets ban. That way you limit their dating options and increase your chances of a second date.

48. Send a wedding invite to every billionaire you can find an address for, as there's a good chance their assistants just send you a gift without ever confirming who you are or if their boss knows you.

49. Tell your kid that if he or she doesn't brush their teeth well enough, they'll all fall out. When they start to lose their baby teeth, tell them they didn't do a good enough job. This way, they'll brush their adult teeth really well.

50. Give the same perfume to your wife and your girlfriend. It could save your ass one day.

51. Give fake money to homeless people. They will thank you for it, but also when they get arrested and taken to jail, it'll reduce the number of homeless people in your area.

52. Don't want to spend a small fortune on a wedding ring? Buy an old wedding ring at a pawn shop and say that it was your grandmother's ring. This will give it more sentiment and value than a new ring.

53. Lie about having a college degree. Companies rarely check them and if they do the only consequence is that they don't hire you.

54. If you can't get your roommate to clean up, create a fake Tinder profile, match with them and tell them you're coming over. They'll leave the place spotless in no time.

55. Starting at a new job? Make sure not to give 100% on your first day. Always give 75%. That way, if you play it down at 50% they'll think you're just having a bad day, and if you later start giving 100% you'll be more likely to get a raise for your improved work effort.

56. If a meeting is getting too boring, stand up and walk out *quickly* while staring at your phone. Nobody will stop you, and you'll have time to think of a decent excuse before you're interrogated.

57. On most graphing calculators you can archive a program or cheat sheet, and when your teacher erases the RAM before a test you can simply go into the archive that wasn't wiped and restore the cheat sheet.

58. If your family or roommates don't want to upgrade internet speed just go into the router admin settings and set their devices to one of the lowest bandwidths possible. When they start complaining about it just tell them that upgrading internet will fix the problem.

59. Did you get the dreaded SSSS on your boarding pass? Just throw it away and pull up your boarding pass on your phone.

60. When planting plants on top of dead bodies, make sure to plant an endangered species so it will be against the law to dig it up.

61. Drug tests at work? Bring homemade food for the office with slight amounts of THC. They can't fire everyone.

62. Take a picture of yourself every day or every week slowly getting fatter and when you've reached a good heavy, post all the photos in reverse along with whatever diet or exercise plan you are selling.

63. If you suspect the apartment next door is an Airbnb, rent it for a night to get the Wi-Fi password and never pay for internet again.

64. If you want people to stop letting their dogs shit on your lawn, put up a "Lawn Recently Treated with Toxic Pesticides" sign. Nobody wants their pet walking around on or accidentally ingesting poison.

65. Break off the end of any random key in your possession and use it as a prop/proof as to why your late for any obligation (work, social, family) by telling them "My stupid key broke off in my door. Had to call a locksmith."

66. College student looking for a wealthy significant other? Go to your schools Top Parental Donors page then locate and seduce their kids.

67. If LDS missionaries knock on your door, ask them to do some manual labor tasks you've been putting off. The church encourages them to help when asked.

68. If you want to rummage through someone's desk drawers and are wary of being caught, do so with an empty stapler in your hand. If confronted just act like you are looking for some staples.

69. Want telemarketers to stop calling you? Sexually harass them.

70. When going in for an interview, make 2 or 3 of your friends to sign up for an interview as well and tell them to give the stupidest interview ever.

71. Need a free phone and / or cash? Volunteer to clean up after a big concert. People tend to lose their stuff there.

72. A little paint on the visor of a riot helmet will render them entirely useless.

73. Tell your kid that they snore in their sleep often, that way you'll know if they're pretending to sleep because they'll fake snore.

74. When going for a new job, tell them you earn more than you currently do but you're "happy to stay at your current salary". They'll usually give you a little bit more anyway, so you'll get a nice raise for yourself.

75. Tired of people driving badly in your area? Grab a random picture of a child off the internet and place it down with some flowers by the side of the road.

76. Buy expensive items and place them around your house. Take a video camera and spend 10min filming every room and every item in your house.

Return the items to the store. If you are ever in the unfortunate situation of a house-fire this will make insurance fraud a thousand times easier.

77. Want your kids to become good liars? Overreact about every little thing they do growing up.

78. Need to trespass? Bring a dog leash. If anyone asks why you are on their property you can tell them you are just looking for your dog.

79. If your mail service loses your mail a lot, keep sending letters to yourself but insure them. It costs about $10 to insure for $300 so if the courier service loses your mail more than 1 times out of 30, you're making money.

80. If you work in an office where your coworkers can't see you enter, don't say good morning to them as soon as you walk in. This way when you are late, they won't know and will just think you haven't come to say good morning yet.

81. Selling a vehicle? Stop into a very nice neighborhood to take pictures. Buyers will be more interested to buy a vehicle from classy people who have money to keep it maintained.

82. Don't feel like working today? Reserve a room for a meeting, play some low-quality jazz music from your phone and if anyone asks what you're doing, just act frustrated and say you're stuck on hold.

83. Leave negative reviews for your gym to deter people from joining and overcrowding the place.

84. Take a picture of your luggage with as much cash as possible so if an airline loses it you could get extra money, as you have photo evidence of money being in the luggage.

85. Worried you may be speaking to an undercover cop? Ask them to perform a sexual favor for you. A member of law enforcement will decline immediately.

86. Find and befriend your co-workers that don't drink, because if there's ever a work function with drink tickets, you can try to get theirs.

87. Lie as badly as you can. For example, act like it's hard to make eye contact, keep a straight face, not laugh, etc. Then, when you actually need to cover something up, it's much easier for someone to believe your lies because you're an "awful liar."

88. If you want to call in sick and need a certificate from the doctor, you can often triple the duration of your certificate by telling the doctor that you're working in the food industry.

89. Win internet arguments by editing your comments after your opponent has responded to completely change what you said and making it look like your opponent has no idea what they're talking about.

90. If you need to lie about something, include an embarrassing unnecessary detail. After all, why would you intentionally lie to make yourself look bad?

91. Having an affair? Change your lover's contact name in your phone to "Scam Likely," so your primary partner won't question why you're getting so many calls.

92. If you're terminally ill and not married, you might as well spend your last few months getting credit cards and running them up to maximize your quality of life.

93. Most counties have lower retirement ages for women. Men simply change your gender at the required age and claim your pension earlier. You can always return to being a man once you're at the male retirement age.

94. If you have spare time at the airport, check the flight monitor for flights that are extremely delayed and walk over to those gates. Airlines will often provide free snacks and beverages for people with delayed flights. Pretend you are a passenger on that flight and enjoy the free snacks.

95. If you are creating a fake profile to interact with something, use an AI generated face as the display picture.

96. Do you and your partner want to visit historic places but can't afford the entrance fee? Pretend you're engaged and are considering the location as your wedding venue. You'll get in for free and be given a tour.

97. Buying something second-hand online? Create multiple accounts to use. One where you will offer the amount you wish to pay, and all the others to offer way less to make the seller think that yours is the best offer.

98. Need a stock photo without the watermark? Do a reverse image search and scroll through to find it on an article. Media companies usually buy the image and upload it on articles.

99. Invite your annoying friends when you know they can't go. It's a great excuse when they complain about never getting invited to stuff.

100.   Want to eavesdrop on someone? AirPods have a "Live Listen" feature that turns your iPhone into a microphone. Leave your phone charging in the room you want to snoop in on and listen in remotely. This works with ear buds on Android phones too.

This list was made in great part from the most popular posts on https://www.reddit.com/r/UnethicalLifeProTips/ It is a great resource for keeping up with new and updated Unethical Life Hacks and Pro Tips.

With Great Power
Comes Great Responsibility

May these pages serve as a catalyst for rethinking the rules we live by, whether you ultimately choose to exploit their loopholes or seek to strengthen them. True power doesn't come from simply knowing how to bend systems to your will; it comes from deciding, with clarity and self-awareness, which boundaries to respect and which to challenge. Whichever path you follow, let your actions be guided by an honest reckoning of consequences, a deliberate understanding of who might be harmed or helped, and a steadfast sense of who you truly want to be in a world where the lines between right and wrong are never as clear as we pretend they are.